ALFRED de MUSSET

by

Margaret A. Rees

This study re-examines the commonly held image of Musset himself and of his work, attempting to show at what points it is out of focus and so presents an over-simplified and diminished picture. After a biographical chapter which sketches in the personality and the experience in which the works are rooted, the book discusses Musset's writings in what is perhaps their ascending order of greatness — his short stories followed by his poetry, and finally by his theater. At the same time Musset's development is traced from the sometimes melodramatic though brilliant pastiches of his debut to the début to the restrained yet even more brilliant masterpieces of his maturity. For the author these pages represent a re-appraisal of a long-held admiration and reach the conclusion that, unlike some idols erected early in life, this one at least does not have feet of clay.

TWAYNE'S WORLD AUTHORS SERIES

A Survey of the World's Literature

Sylvia E. Bowman, Indiana University

GENERAL EDITOR

FRANCE

Maxwell A. Smith, Guerry Professor of French, Emeritus
The University of Chattanooga
Former Visiting Professor in Modern Languages
The Florida State University

EDITOR

Alfred de Musset

(TWAS 137)

TWAYNE'S WORLD AUTHORS SERIES (TWAS)

*The purpose of TWAS is to survey the major writers—
novelists, dramatists, historians, poets, philosophers,
and critics—of the nations of the world. Among the
national literatures covered are those of Australia,
Canada, China, Eastern Europe, France, Germany,
Greece, India, Italy, Japan, Latin America, New
Zealand, Poland, Russia, Scandinavia, Spain, and the
African nations, as well as Hebrew, Yiddish, and
Latin Classical literatures. This survey is comple-
mented by Twayne's United States Authors Series
and English Authors Series.*

*The intent of each volume in these series is to present
a critical-analytical study of the works of the writer;
to include biographical and historical material that
may be necessary for understanding, appreciation,
and critical appraisal of the writer; and to present all
material in clear, concise English—but not to vitiate
the scholarly content of the work by doing so.*

Alfred de Musset

By MARGARET A. REES

Former Dudin Brown Scholar
of Westfield College,
University of London

Twayne Publishers, Inc.   ::   New York

Library of Congress Catalog Card Number: 73-120495

ABOUT THE AUTHOR

Margaret A. Rees *(née* Williams) studied at Westfield College in the University of London, where she was Senior Scholar of her year and twice won a College essay prize. She undertook a postgraduate study of Spain in nineteenth-century French literature and obtained the M.A. in 1956 and the Ph.D. in 1959, having been awarded a London University Research Studentship, then a Leverhulme Fellowship at the University of Liverpool, where she had taught in the Hispanic and French departments. She has contributed articles on topics in both those fields, and especially on France-Spanish literary relations during the Romantic period, to journals appearing in Britain, France, Spain, and the U.S. She is currently preparing an edition of Alfred de Musset's *Contes d'Espagne et d'Italie.*

AMERICA

To my parents

Preface

ed
of
me
ad
sm
yes
on
a

ent
hat
the
nan
the
nd
ove
him
be
but
to
stly
ble

of a
ive,
ued
tail
ngs,
to
any
s in
ater
his

ALFRED de MUSSET

gifts. I have tried to limit to the minimum general discussions of the literary scene to which Musset belonged. It was often a temptation to dwell on this background at greater length, but to do so would have meant misappropriating space needed for the main subject; I also felt that such material might be out of place in a study forming part of a series which itself constitutes a panoramic view of French literature.

Preparing this book has given me the chance to carry out a personal investigation, the re-exploration of an enthusiasm for Musset which did indeed begin at seventeen but which resolutely refused to disappear with adolescence, as some academics believe that it should. Far from fading under the light of re-examination, this admiration is still growing stronger. Those who are allergic to Musset will object that such a process could happen only to intellectual Peter Pans, but I have tried to show in the following pages how much food for thought as well as esthetic enjoyment he offers. Nevertheless, genuine liking must be aware of limitations as infatuation is not, and the concluding chapter in particular tries to delineate the narrow boundaries of the world Musset creates.

Any student knows that in some ways it is easier to write adverse criticism rather than praise, but I would urge those who find my claims on Musset's behalf excessive to turn back to the texts themselves, for he can speak far more convincingly for himself than can any commentator. In particular, where translations of his poetry are given, I would ask readers to look on these purely as tools intended to help those who may find them useful to return to the original as quickly as they can. Translating verse can be a rewarding exercise, but with Musset it is as difficult as trying to capture the essence of Parisian air in a bottle for export. Unless otherwise stated, all quotations from Musset's works are taken from Philippe Van Tieghem's edition of his *Œuvres complètes* in the series entitled *Collection L'Intégrale* (Paris: Editions du Seuil, 1963).

I should like to express my gratitude to my family, whose unfailing help has made it possible for me to work on this book, and especially to my husband for the patience with which he has put his bibliographical and typographical knowledge at my disposal. Lastly, I am glad to acknowledge with affectionate admiration my debt to the late Madame A. M. Danson for her inspiring teaching of nineteenth-century French literature in general and of Musset's work in particular.

MARGARET A. REES

Leeds, England

Contents

Chronology

1810 Louis-Charles-Alfred de Musset born in Paris, December 11.
1819 Musset becomes a pupil at the Lycée (then "Collège") Henri IV.
1827 In the "Concours général" he is awarded the second prize for a Latin essay, the first prize in philosophy, and the second prize for a French essay.
1828 Follows university courses in law and medicine for a short time, but then decides to concentrate on the study of art. He is introduced into the Romantic *cénacle* whose leader is Victor Hugo, and also makes friends among the elegant young men of Parisian high society.
1829 His father finds him work in the office of a firm of military heating contractors, but the publication in December of the *Premières Poésies* (dated 1830) allows him to leave this post and devote himself to his career as a writer.
1830 *La Quittance du Diable* written but not performed. First performance of *La Nuit vénitienne* in December a catastrophic failure.
1831 Musset's "Revues fantastiques" appear from January to June in *Le Temps*.
1832 Alfred's father dies. *Un Spectacle dans un fauteuil* published in December, bearing the date of the following year.
1833 *André del Sarto* published in April and *Les Caprices de Marianne* in May. At a dinner given for collaborators of the *Revue des Deux Mondes* in June Musset meets George Sand, and by the end of July they are lovers. On December 12 they leave for Italy, arriving in Venice on December 30.
1834 *Fantasio* appears in January. Early in February Musset falls dangerously ill with malarial fever in Venice and, while still convalescent, discovers that George has come to love his doctor, Pagello. On March 29 he sets off alone for Paris. *On ne badine pas avec l'amour* published in July and *Lorenzaccio* in August. On August 14 George Sand returns to France, bringing Pagello with her; Musset leaves for Baden on August 22. When he comes

back to Paris in October he and George try to take up their life together again, but their relationship consists of a series of violent quarrels and reconciliations.

1835   Musset and George Sand finally separate. Musset has a brief affair with Madame Jaubert, the *marraine* who remains his friend long after they cease to be lovers. *La Nuit de mai* and *La Nuit de décembre* written during this year. Publication in August of *La Quenouille de Barberine;* of *La Confession d'un enfant du siècle* (part I, ch. 3) in the following month; and of *Le Chandelier* in November.

1836   Liaison with Louise Lebrun, an actress. In February, publication of *La Confession d'un enfant du siècle* in its entirety; in March, *Lettre à Lamartine;* in July, *Il ne faut jurer de rien;* in August, *La Nuit d'août;* in September, the first of the *Lettres de Dupuis et Cotonet.*

1837   Musset's liaison with Aimée d'Alton begins in April, lasting until November, 1838. Publication of *La Nuit d'octobre, Un Caprice,* and two stories, *Emmeline* and *Les Deux Maîtresses.*

1838   Three short stories published: *Frédéric et Bernerette, Le Fils du Titien,* and *Margot.* Musset appointed librarian at the Ministère de l'Intérieur.

1839   The singer, Pauline Garcia, does not respond to Musset's advances, but Rachel, the Racinian actress, becomes his mistress. *Croisilles* published in February.

1840   Musset, suffering from a severe attack of pleurisy, is nursed by a nun, Sister Marcelline, for whom he comes to feel great affection. First edition of his *Poésies complètes* and of the *Comédies et Proverbes.*

1841   *Souvenir* published in February.

1842   The Princess Belgiojoso reacts coldly to Musset's courtship. *Histoire d'un merle blanc* appears in October.

1843   In January Musset is gravely ill once more. Friends hope to marry him to the daughter of the playwright, Mélesville, but the plan comes to nothing. *Pierre et Camille* published in April. Musset spends several days in prison for having neglected his duties as a member of the National Guard.

1844   Following a pattern which is to be repeated in 1845, the early months of the year bring a fresh bout of severe illness to Musset. *Le Secret de Javotte* is published in June and *Les Frères Van Buck* in July.

1845   Musset becomes a Chevalier de la Légion d'Honneur. *Il faut qu'une porte soit ouverte ou fermée* published in November and the short story, *Mimi Pinson,* in December.

1847   For the first time a play of Musset's is performed at the Comédie-Française, largely due to the efforts of an actress, Madame Allan-Despréaux: *Un Caprice* has its first night in November.

1848   Musset persuades Madame Allan-Despréaux to become his mistress. In May his appointment as librarian is abruptly canceled.

1849   Performance of *Louison,* and of *On ne saurait penser à tout.*

1850   In November-December *Carmosine* is published.

1851   *Bettine* performed in October and published in November.

1852   Musset elected to the Académie. For six months he and Louise Colet, the poet, are lovers. Definitive editions of the *Premières Poésies* and the *Poésies nouvelles.*

1853   Musset appointed librarian at the Ministère de l'Instruction Publique. The first part of *La Mouche* appears in December, to be completed early in the New Year.

1854   Complete edition of the *Comédies et Proverbes.*

1855   *L'Ane et le ruisseau* written.

1856   Musset's last *nouvelle, Les Amours du petit Job et de la belle Blandine,* published.

1857   Musset dies on May 2 and is buried in the cemetery of Père-Lachaise.

CHAPTER 1

Le Prince Phosphore-
de-Coeur-Volant

*"Il aimait sentir autour de lui une
atmosphère de tendresse et d'affection;
c'était même chez lui un besoin."*[1]

I *The Enigma*

THE life of a nineteenth-century writer, amply documented with all
kinds of material and studied by critic after critic, ought surely to
present a perfectly clear picture, one would think. Yet, after over a
hundred years of commentary, Philippe Soupault can still write that it
is useless to search in the many biographies of Musset for a true picture
of the man who was one of the greatest authors of his century.[2] The
difficulty does not lie in tracing the outline of Musset's life. His
comings and goings, which were few since he preferred above all "this
boring city of Paris, which I adore,"[3] and even the pattern of his
everyday life—his favorite cafés and his circle of acquaintances—can be
discovered from his correspondence, the memoirs of his contemporaries
and, potentially most promising, his brother's biography of him. If one
could be set down in the Paris of those days, few literary figures would
be easier to locate at any given moment than Musset, given these guides.
The only gaps in our information are tantalizing ones—Musset's
whereabouts on those days, sometimes several at a time, when he
disappeared so completely in the maze of Parisian lowlife that neither
his mother nor his current mistress had any idea of where he was.

Yet in spite of all the facts that can be amassed, Musset himself
remains more of an enigma than his enigmatic creation, Lorenzaccio.
Barbey d'Aurevilly, commenting on his disappointment with Paul de
Musset's biography of his brother, wrote that the real story of this life
was enacted, unseen by the world, within the narrow bounds of
Alfred's frame, its crises unknown even to those closest to him[4] and,
while this could no doubt be applied to most human beings, it seems so
particularly true of Alfred de Musset that one despairs of catching sight

of his real personality, whose chameleon changefulness makes it all the more elusive. The other nickname Madame Jaubert bestowed on her "Prince Phosphore-de-cœur-volant" was "le prince Café ... because he was continually in motion, exciting to watch, to listen to, mentally stimulating even in his way of listening"; and it was she who wrote of him: "No stormy sky, streaked with cloud and lit by a March sun can compare for changeability with his moods."[5]

Descriptions of his appearance, first when he was introduced into the Romantic *cénacle,* then in 1830, and finally when he was in his forties, make it clear that the drama which took place in the secret theater within him must have rivaled the events of any Classical tragedy in its terrible ravages. In a portrait of him during his early days in the Romantic *cénacle,* Sainte-Beuve depicts a youth who seemed to typify adolescent genius, his brow proud and manly, the bloom of childhood still on his cheeks, his nostrils flaring with eagerness. "As he came forward, his footsteps rang out and his gaze ranged high, as though he were certain of victory and full of the pride of life." Lamartine paints a less martial portrait, but still one which might be that of the ideal Romantic hero. To his eyes, Musset was a handsome young man with long, lustrous hair; the brow of a dreamer rather than a thinker; eyes too which were dreamy rather than sparkling; and an extremely sensitive mouth hesitating between sadness and a smile; a tall, supple frame which seemed too slight to bear even the light burden of his few years.[6] Two years later, in 1830, a guest at Alfred de Vigny's salon describes Musset as a young man, elegantly dressed in the very height of fashion—a frock coat with a velvet collar reaching to the waist and tightly fitting sky-blue trousers—and comments on his regular, handsome features, but already there was something in Musset's expression which made him think, in suitably Romantic terms, of "a beautiful flower which has been plucked and has faded before evening."[7]

During the last seventeen years or so of his life, the Musset whom his old acquaintances met in the haunts of Parisian society was reduced to far more of a shadow of this golden youth than the passage of time warranted. Pierre Gastinel in his book *Le Romantisme d'Alfred de Musset* (Paris, 1933) has used many contemporary memoirs to form a composite picture. His ash-blond hair, gleaming when the street- or café-lights played on it, might still have been the envy of any woman, but the face beneath it was prematurely lined, and strikingly thin and pale. His lower lip now gave an impression of weakness, as though he were in a stupor, and his usually wide-open eyes seemed at times to contract as if trying to narrow their range. Sometimes his expression was unmistakably that of a drunkard, but more often it bore the stamp of a painful melancholy, a look of "weakness, gloom, weariness . . . with something of the despair of a drowning man." Yet it was still an arresting face, combining distinction and delicacy of feature with a tortured look in a way which reminded some acquaintances of a Renaissance profile. Musset was still slim and elegantly dressed, with something of the dash of an officer of the "Hussards," but now his bearing had a stiff and stilted quality about it which reminded one commentator of a typical Englishman's manner. "He seemed to be keeping a close rein on himself as though he could not trust himself." Even his voice was weaker, his very enunciation less clear, and in company, although there were flashes of his old charm, he was for the most part plunged in a scornful, misanthropic silence (See Gastinel, pp. 602-603).

Barbey d'Aurevilly has a twofold explanation for this wreck of youthful brilliance, an explanation generally accepted even in our own day. In his essay he speaks first of "this young genius who tore himself to shreds on all the pleasures of mad youth" and then of "Alfred de Musset, that immortal lover of women now dead, made happy by all of them, suffering through one alone and finally dying because of her" *(op. cit.,* pp. 278 and 279). Debauchery and George Sand, much though Musset's conscience was tormented by the one and his memory haunted by the other, make up too simple a solution to the problem. The search for the true solution has an interest wider than the attempt to understand one enigmatic individual. Barbey d'Aurevilly sees Musset as "the poet who was the essence of the soul and the youth of us all" and, in a context larger even than that of his own generation, believes his genius to be "the most powerfully human and the most powerfully modern—the fullest representative of *us all* in fact, who has . . . ever existed" (pp. 271 and 281). Most present-day students of French literature, except perhaps for those who had made a special study of Musset, would probably greet this assertion with scorn, but Barbey d'Aurevilly's feeling that the generation which was young in 1830 was somehow personified in Musset is surely worth an examination which may even show that his wider claim also has some truth in it.

II *Ancestry and Childhood*

Léon Séché, in the first volume of his study on Alfred de Musset in the series *Etudes d'histoire romantique* (Paris, 1907. See pp. 13-66), explores Musset's family background with an infectious enthusiasm, describing in the early pages how at the break of day he traveled through the countryside around Vendôme to see the manor of Bonnaventure, which came into the hands of the Musset family in the sixteenth century through the marriage of Claude de Musset, "lieutenant-général" of the province of Blois, to the daughter of the lord of Bonnaventure. Alfred himself was the last owner of the estate, and he finally sold it. Unlike most of his ancestors, he was born not at Bonnaventure but in Paris, at 33 rue des Noyers (the street disappeared long ago). Nevertheless, this Parisian par excellence was not cut off from his family's roots in the Vendômois countryside. Paul tells how he and Alfred spent several days staying at Bonnaventure in 1822, and we have a sketch of the manor house which Alfred is said to have made when he was twelve years old.[8]

Séché is convinced that the key to much in Alfred's temperament and physical traits is to be found among his forebears. In many ways it was an ancestry calculated to fire the imagination of any young boy, especially one with literary leanings. The Mussets of the sixteenth century, bearing their arms of azure with a golden sparrow hawk and the device "Courtoisie Bonne-Aventure aux preux" (or "aux preuses"), bring a glimpse both of the revelries and the outpouring of poetry associated with the Renaissance. Ronsard is said to have known the Claude de Musset who married the lord of Bonnaventure's daughter, and certainly in 1707 Alfred's great-grandfather married Marguerite-Angélique du Bellay, directly descended from cousins of the poet Joachim du Bellay, who turned his sufferings in Italy into literary masterpieces just as Alfred de Musset was to do. The Mussets are also said to have been joined in marriage to a family related to Joan of Arc and Alfred is quoted as claiming in the midst of a dinner party, whether jestingly or not, that Joan was his "great-great-aunt." Both these were dazzling ornaments for a family tree, but a third shone with a partly tarnished luster. Some six generations before Alfred, Cassandra Salviati, the inspiration for many of Ronsard's poems, became a Musset by marriage and, although her name is still bright with the glory with which poetry had surrounded it, critics claim that it was through her that the tainted blood of the womanizing, wine-besotted sector of Florentine society in the Renaissance became part of Musset's inheritance.

Without a knowledge of genetics, it is difficult to know how reasonable it would be to see in Alfred a "throwback" to his Salviati ancestors. It is true that Paul described his brother as having the face and the soul of a Renaissance Italian, a resemblance brought out in Achille Devéria's portrait of him masquerading as a page from sixteenth-century Italy, and critics such as Séché interpret the loathsome Salviati in *Lorenzaccio* as a somber self-portrait of the author. His mixed heredity has been blamed for his weakness for prostitutes and alcohol as well as for his mastery of poetry but, in a period when the exotic South was immensely fashionable and Victor Hugo liked to think of himself as being almost an adopted Spaniard because his father had been made a grandee, Musset himself seemed to lay no great stress on the streak of Italian blood in his veins. Even a purely French ancestry would have been no guarantee against an inherited tendency to libertinage and, as we shall see, he had other characteristics, such as his clear-eyed raillery of deviations from the norm of good sense, which are usually labeled traditionally French.

The hypersensitivity of emotions and senses which later helped to make life almost intolerable for him can be seen already in his early years. The golden-haired child whose cherubic smile seems placid enough in portraits was in fact a bundle of nerves and could be swung from laughter to tears by the slightest change in circumstances; while he was still a boy there were times when he would see his own double—a kind of ghostly twin—appear beside him. By the time he was old enough to handle a gun, an accident occurred whose aftermath followed a pattern recurring throughout his adult life. A shot from his gun landed uncomfortably close to Paul, and the shock plunged Alfred rather than the near-victim into an attack of nerves followed by a bout of fever.

As far as his highly charged emotions would allow, his childhood seems to have been an exceptionally happy one, surrounded by comfort and affection from the December day when he was born, as Charpentier describes it, in the cosy atmosphere of a room made cheerful by a bright log fire. (Born in December, Charpentier writes, he died in May, the month of roses, and in his life there was neither summer nor autumn, but only spring and winter.)[9] The enveloping comfort of the fire-lit room where he was born was replaced by the enveloping affection of his parents—his father a witty man of charm and intelligence, then in his fifties and an author in his own right; his mother the personification of gentleness. No doubt trying to cushion their younger son against the extremes of his own temperament, they brought him up with a leniency which to some biographers seems outrageous spoiling, and even his elder brother constantly protected him from the consequences of his moments of wildness. Perhaps one of the saddest notes in his last years is the continued dependence of a highly intelligent man of considerable integrity and pride on his family and finally on his housekeeper, on those who were familiar with the alarms and illnesses to which his taut nerves left him exposed, and who were fond enough of him either to ward them off or nurse him though them.

Often-repeated anecdotes tell of a child avid for affection and generous in bestowing it, a fitting prelude to Musset's adult search for human love and beauty. At four years of age, we are told, he fidgeted constantly on his mother's knee at a wedding breakfast, explaining that he was trying to look at the bride's beautiful white neck. Probably his first great passion was for his cousin Clélie whom he asked to marry him when he was old enough. Her eventual marriage was kept secret from him for a while, but when he discovered it, the small boy forgave her, after first making sure with his characteristic touchiness that she had never made fun of his offered love. Perhaps the best-known anecdote relates how Alfred as a very young child was given a new pair of red shoes which delighted him and how he fumed with impatience for his mother to take him out to show them off. In his "Hurry, hurry, maman, or my new shoes will be old already," critics see signs of his eager impetuosity as a man to sample all life's pleasures as quickly as possible.

Almost any childhood can provide striking or precocious sayings, and perhaps it is biographers' tales of the early experiences which furnished his mind and memory which are of most interest to Alfred's readers. Paul tells us how his grandfather Guyot-Desherbiers and a great-aunt lived only two houses away from his own and had a garden stretching as far as the nearby church (later destroyed), so that all the grandchildren had the advantage over most Parisian children in having the run of a garden of their own. It would be strange if this garden—combining with later experiences—played no part in Musset's exquisite garden scenes, such as that which precedes Brigitte's surrender to Octave in *La Confession d'un enfant du siècle*, and in the tissue of images drawn from nature found throughout most of his works. Musset never attempts the detailed, informed portraits of nature of a John Clare or a Kathleen Raine, but for a self-avowed devotee of Paris his works are surprisingly refreshed with trees, flowers, and green lawns.

Through Paul's biography we know too of the hero worship of Napoleon which the boys caught from their mother, their sense of utter catastrophe when they heard of his defeat at Waterloo, and the suffering endured for their political sympathies at the school where Paul was a boarder and Alfred a day boy. So ultra-royalist was this school that the most aristocratic pupil sat at a desk of his own in front of an unused door which was covered with magnificent blue paper decorated with golden fleurs-de-lis. Fortunately, the scarlet fever rescued them from this classroom and gave them the leisure to explore the fantastic world of *The Thousand and One Nights.* The two convalescents acted out the stories, first rigging up an Oriental palace-cum-grotto reached by twenty steps, the lowest a music book and the highest a writing desk. The door was a large volume which could be opened by pulling a cord passed through the broken binding. The "back door" was a long polished plank leading to a soft landing on a mattress, and this exit was used for speedy escapes, aerial flights, and the sudden appearance of the genie of the lamp. In *Madrid, Don Paez,* and even *Fantasio* Musset was still constructing magical palaces and cities but, perhaps because he had already had his fill of exoticism as a boy, he was not for long the victim of the Oriental mania which gripped so many Romantics. With his brother too he relived the medieval tales of chivalry, finally falling out of love with them in a way that would have delighted Cervantes—by reading *Don Quixote.*

For about two years the children enjoyed their freedom under the wing of a friendly young tutor, M. Bouvrain, who managed to instruct them while they thought they were playing, giving them history lessons as they walked near the forest of Carnelles, in the neighborhood of the country house loaned to their parents. It was from this tutor that they also acquired the knowledge of Italian that was to be so valuable to them, learning it not from books but by conversing. It was only when M. Bouvrain wished to leave his post and no satisfactory replacement was found that the boys were sent to the famous Collège (now Lycée) Henri IV, Paul as a boarder and Alfred, then nine years old, as a day boy.

For Alfred, the change was a reversal of fortunes. He made his first appearance still wearing the long golden curls which would have entranced most mothers but which provoked a barrage of jeers from his classmates; nor did his long lace collar help. These were matters easily put right, but more trouble was in store. The high standard of his work had earned him a place in a class where he was the smallest boy in size, and the rest of the class was infuriated to see this golden-haired mother's darling being awarded such high grades that the headmaster offered him a free boarding place in his own house as a prospective prize winner in the state examinations. Madame de Musset refused the offer, thinking that too much study might be bad for his health, but before Alfred could escape to his home each day he had to fight his way across a great courtyard, through two lines of schoolboys bent on showing with their fists how much they disapproved of such brilliance in someone younger. Paul relates that for over a month his younger brother would reach the gate with his clothes torn and often with his face bleeding, until the day when an older friend saw what was happening and attacked the persecutors so fiercely that they never ambushed him again.

Alfred kept his place near the head of his class, without ever needing to overwork. He was so anxious to please that he was inconsolable on one occasion when he did not win his usual place on the "bench of honor"; and he made such progress that he would have completed the school course at fifteen if he had not repeated the senior year, "la classe de philosophie." It was here, according to Paul, that he first gave signs of an original, questioning mind that fully assimilated the arguments put to him but was dissatisfied until he had rethought the question for himself and reached his own conclusions. In very much the same way, he later penetrated the Romantic citadel of Victor Hugo's group only to subject its trends to the clear-sighted appraisal which led him away from it.

The school career that had begun with a bedraggled nine-year-old boy battling his way daily across the courtyard among the blows and taunts of his classmates ended as he mounted the platform to carry off the second prize for a Latin essay in a competition open to all *collèges*. He was sixteen, but still so slight and so young for his class that the *grand-maître de l'Université* could not help smiling as he saw the small boy who was coming forward to accept one of the major prizes. It would have been the first prize if the examiners had not disagreed as to whether Alfred's essay had paid enough attention to the religious side of the question he dealt with, and if the casting vote had not belonged to the *grand-maître,* who was a bishop.

At the end of his schooldays we hear, for the first time, his own voice speaking, in two letters which he wrote while he was on holiday staying with his grandfather at the Château de Cogners, between Le Mans and Vendôme. Biographer after biographer quotes these letters for the good reason that they throw an amazingly accurate beam of light on to the way in which his character and career were to develop. "I am bored and depressed," he writes in the first letter. "I should like to be a Shakespeare or a Schiller or else not to write at all, and so I do nothing! I believe that the greatest misfortune that can befall a man of strong emotions is to feel none. ... I would give away my life for twopence if one did not have to pass through death to leave it." Romantic weariness with life is combined with Romantic idealism and sense of the contrasts which make up mankind, but Musset seems sincere in expressing these feelings, whereas so many contemporaries adopted them as a pose. "The same breath gives us life, why did He who gave it to us leave it so imperfect? I cannot endure this mingling of joy and sadness, this fusion of earthly mire with what is heavenly." He continues: Why should nature have made him thirst for an unattainable ideal? He cannot believe that his dreams should really be beyond his grasp, and he is convinced that both he and his correspondent, Paul Foucher, are intended to be something more than respectable, clever attorneys.

Already he sees love as a refuge from unhappiness—"I need a dainty foot and a slender waist; I need someone to love"—or, failing love, alcohol—"If I were in Paris now I should drown all that is left of my finer feelings in punch and beer, and my troubles would be eased. A sick man is given opium to make him sleep even though the sleep may be fatal for him. I should do the same with my soul." These words, written on September 23, 1827, read like a somber presage of the last seventeen years of his life.

The second letter, dated October 19, includes a penetrating comment on his poetry, a comment which again foretells the future. "With me, poetry is the sister of love. The one gives rise to the other, and they always arrive together. When I lose the ability to fall in love as easily as I catch cold, I shall never again feel this desire [to write poetry]." They say that Puccini, too, never composed unless he was in love. Again and again the letter returns to the theme of his restless longing. "I am not in love . . . but I am certain that I was made to be in love. . . . I play billiards like a madman . . . I have a need for excess of some sort or another. . . . I don't know how to shake off this need of emotion. . . . Perhaps this Winter I shall find a wife, . . . and then! . . . what does anything else matter to me? . . . If I found the woman I am looking for . . ., then I should stop in my tracks and say: 'That is the end of my career!' "

Many young men in their late teens must have written or felt in much the same way in every century, especially those who found themselves as Musset did in a limbo between the end of their schooldays and the start of some as yet undecided career. Most of them, twenty years or so later, would have turned into the respectable, worthy career men mentioned in the first letter, but the strange thing about Musset's adolescent letters, as about his childish sayings, is the extreme degree to which their sentiments persisted and even increased in the adult man. With him, youthful idealism and intensity of feeling never fizzled out into comfortable compromise with what was possible.

III *The Romantic* Cénacle *and Musset's Early Publications*

A few months later, thanks to Paul's biography, we catch a glimpse of Alfred strolling through the Bois de Boulogne in the springtime, on his leisurely way back to Auteuil where his mother had taken an apartment. He belonged now to the band of students whom he was to describe in his short stories, but he still felt no calling to any particular career or even subject, and the frequency with which he changed his course would have broken the heart of any modern university dean. Law he found arid, and his medical studies lasted no longer than the nausea of his first dissection class. In despair at his lack of a vocation, he shut himself in his room for several days, emerging to declare that man was limited enough as it was and that he could never resign himself to the restrictions of any particular profession.

Nevertheless, he was cheered when his art teacher told him that he was gifted enough to become an artist if he chose, and from then on he would set off daily for Paris to spend his time at the Louvre or in his master's studio. Far from nature playing an unimportant part in Musset's work, as some critics say, the Bois de Boulogne as he walked home to Auteuil with a book for companion provided him with an ideal setting for the discovery of his real vocation. Paul tells that one evening Alfred returned later than usual because, immersed in a volume of Chénier's poems, he had taken the longest way home. His own first poem (apart from one he had written for his mother's birthday when he was fourteen) was sparked off by this reading of Chénier, and its hundred or so lines came to him as he walked home on two successive days. He did not think this poem worth keeping, and his first short play also found its way into the fire.

This, too, had taken shape beneath the chestnut trees of the Bois, but it had been inspired not by his reading but by the works he had heard declaimed at Victor Hugo's house where Paul Foucher had taken him. Here, or at the gatherings at the Arsenal library where Charles Nodier was curator, he met the vanguard of writers who were determined to destroy Classicism in a literary equivalent of the storming of the Bastille. Artistic freedom was one of the battlecries of the group. The author must be free to explore all the possibilities of his subject according to his own inspiration, and not be bound by literary regulations governing vocabulary, versification, construction, the nature of the plot, the choice of theme, and the range of characters. The individual artist, not the Classical canons of good taste, was now to be the arbiter of the content and form of his creation.

Perhaps there has never been a literary school so easy to ridicule as the Romantic group. Its enthusiasms and its stress on the individual sometimes led its members into excesses which are a gift to the caricaturist and the writer of parodies, but that should not make us forget the heady atmosphere of the world into which Musset entered. Théophile Gautier describes how it seemed as though color and lyricism, muted and restrained by the pseudo-Classics, came flooding back into art with the second renaissance that was the Romantic movement. In 1843, in his *Réponse à M. Charles Nodier,* Musset looks back wistfully to the gaiety of these evenings when, naturally enough since almost all the guests were young, the reading of new works and the hammering out of new literary theories was interrupted by most people taking the floor to dance as Marie Nodier's fingers flew over the keyboard. Sometimes, too, everyone would pour out of the Arsenal to wander through the streets or along the quais, watch the sun set, or climb the towers of Notre-Dame for a panoramic view over the city.

Following chapters will try to disentangle the relationship between Musset's writings and those of the rest of the group, but certainly it was in this hothouse of youthful enthusiasm that his own verses began to flower. He first saw his own lines in print on August 31, 1828, when a Dijon newspaper, *Le Provincial,* published a poem called "Un Rêve," very much in the manner of Victor Hugo. Soon he was reading to the Arsenal gatherings poems which were to be included in the *Contes d'Espagne et d'Italie,* and reaping praise from his audience. To many of them he seemed the incarnation of youthful genius, both in looks and ability. Already his poems bore their own individual stamp. "This poetry had quality and life," wrote Dumas later. "It was neither Lamartine, nor Hugo, nor Vigny; it was a flower from the same garden, it is true; a fruit from the same orchard, true again; but a flower with its own scent, a fruit with its own flavor."[10]

In just as lyrical a vein, Sainte-Beuve described Musset at this time as the very incarnation of springtime and, if it is true that there was no equivalent of Summer in his life, nevertheless these years that span the time from the introduction to the *Cénacle* to his Italian journey form a period that had almost all the glory of a summer's day. Toward his eighteenth birthday a metamorphosis in his manner and appearance took place, and the timid stripling turned into a dashing young man with a gaze so steady and so questioning that even his brother had difficulty in meeting it. What was probably his first love affair of any importance quickly followed this transformation, and now Musset was no longer to be found wandering through the Bois de Boulogne but hurrying across to Saint-Denis to keep his engagements with a young married woman who, most Romantically, was incurably consumptive. Tantalizingly little is known about this affair, and very different valuations have been put upon its effect on Musset. It certainly introduced him to the association of love, deception, and pain which was to recur throughout his life and his writings, for he soon discovered that his mistress, instead of loving him sincerely, was using his attentions as a screen to hide from her husband her relationship with another man. It would not have been surprising if the realization that the woman to whom he had entrusted his love was not merely unfaithful but also calculatingly deceitful and callous had been the starting point of Musset's tragic inability to have wholehearted confidence in the sincerity of any woman. George Sand blamed this failing on his rakish life and tried to convince him that it was the fruit of debauchery, but it seems likely that his first love must share at least some of the blame. Paul brushed aside the incident, maintaining that Alfred gave no sign of either anger or scorn and was soon consoled by the attentions of another woman. Yet *La Confession d'un enfant du siècle* describes how another betrayal (in reality Musset's betrayal by the Marquise de la Carte and Jules Janin) leaves a deep psychological wound, and it is hard to imagine that a very young man as candid, passionate, and sensitive as he was could have escaped unmarked from his first adventure. Seven years later, when he suspected that he had been allocated the same role of *chandelier* or decoy lover he put his younger self into his theater as Fortunio in *Le Chandelier,* making the fictional ending much happier than his own experience with the woman whose name may have been Madame Groisellier.

In 1829 he began to see less of the writers and artists who gathered at the Arsenal. His aristocratic, pleasure-loving tastes were drawing him into the company of the dandies, the "golden youth" of Parisian society whose revels he describes in *Les Deux Maîtresses.* Octave's hour had struck, as Gastinel puts it in terms of *Les Caprices de Marianne,* and, as though he could not wait to drink at a single draught all the pleasures of high society, Musset threw himself into the world of fashionable clothes, gambling, hired horses, and social evenings that continued into the early hours of the morning. The mainly literary world of Hugo's group could not satisfy him, and he justified the apparent folly of living in a style with which his finances could not cope by chalking up the expense to experience. "I want to learn everything by experience and not by hearsay," he replied when Paul remonstrated at the size of his tailor's bills. "I believe that there are two men in me, one a man of action, the other an observer. If the former makes a mistake, the latter will profit by it" *(Biographie d'Alfred de Musset* by Paul de Musset, p. 22 in Van Tieghem's edition of Alfred's *Œuvres complètes).*

He gained more from moving in dandy circles than the knowledge which allows him to depict Octave, the carnival reveler in *Les Caprices de Marianne,* so convincingly. Some of the young men-about-town with whom he associated now had solid qualities as well as superficial glitter and among them rather than among the Romantic writers he found his one or two close and long-term friends. Alfred Tattet especially, whom Musset portrays in the *Confession* under the name of Desgenais, may not have been an ideal companion from some points of view; but until he died, some months before the other Alfred's own death, he showed real concern for his well-being, trying at one time to speed up the final break with George Sand and later deploring the way in which he squandered so much of his time on prostitutes.

Tattet and Ulric Guttinguer, an older man whose experience of life Musset envied, were two of the very few men who knew him intimately. With most women he was candor and spontaneity personi-fied, but men rarely succeeded in penetrating the barrier of reserve with which he surrounded himself in their company. He was well aware of this tendency, and when Madame Jaubert reproached him in later years with his cold reception of overtures of friendship even from men who were both intelligent and goodhearted, he replied that he was indifferent to men in general. In any case, his one trial of close friendship (with Paul Foucher?) had shown him that these were deep waters of feeling in which he did not wish to become involved.[11] Nevertheless, among his new companions he found gaiety and all the enthusiasm for his poetic genius which Hugo's group had already shown. Guttinguer wrote later: "When I read the Contes d'Espagne,/ Like the cork from a bottle of champagne/I leaped into the air."[12]

It was an action of Alfred's father that spurred him on to offer the *Contes d'Espagne et d'Italie* to a publisher. One morning M. de Musset announced that he had found Alfred a clerical post with a firm of military heating contractors. His employers were far from demanding, but his loathing for the work and for his loss of liberty never waned, except momentarily when he collected his salary. Bent on convincing his father that he had no need to sit behind an office desk to earn money, he took his poems to the publisher Urbain Canel, who agreed to print them if Musset would provide the extra five hundred lines needed to make up a volume. Taking a three weeks' summer holiday, he retreated to his uncle's house at Le Mans, and returned triumphant to

Paris with *Mardoche.* Urbain Canel kept his word. On Christmas Eve, 1829, Musset invited to his father's house guests who included Mérimée and Vigny, and who applauded enthusiastically his reading of *Don Paez, Portia,* and *Mardoche.* A few days later the *Contes d'Espagne et d'Italie* appeared in print.

Not all readers were as full of admiration as was his first audience or as was Alexandre Dumas *père,* who later commented that Musset was one of those privileged beings who make their debut with a masterly work. Gastinel, who has made a thorough study of press reactions to the *Contes d'Espagne et d'Italie,* reports that eight out of fifteen reviews were favorable (pp. 131-46), but it was inevitable in 1830 that many critics' views should be colored by the side which they upheld in the campaign for or against the Romantic movement to which the work clearly belonged. Some were so incensed by *Ballade à la lune,* which seemed to them an outrage against poetry, that their rage blinded them to the rest of the poems. Between them the cries of fury and the cries of admiration made the *Contes d'Espagne et d'Italie* a succès de scandale which young poets would envy nowadays when almost any volume of poetry passes unobserved except in strictly literary circles.

Some reviewers wisely advised Musset to listen more closely to his own judgment and to disassociate himself from Romantic exaggerations, and paradoxically, while arguments raged over the content and manner of the newly published poems, he was already moving away from their Romanticism to perfect the individual views and style which were to make him an isolated, independent figure. As early as February 6, 1830, his father commented in a letter that Alfred was becoming "deromanticized," and on September 19 he wrote: "The Romantic is completely dehugotized."[13] This line of development follows, after all, the pattern which Paul noticed in Alfred's study of philosophical dogmas while he was at school. At first, as we said before, he would absorb himself enthusiastically in a doctrine, exploring it thoroughly, but always emerging in the end with his own independent views on the subject.

It is doubtful whether Musset's innate sense of moderation and of the ridiculous—the typically eighteenth-century qualities which critics note in him—ever let him close his eyes to the defects of Romanticism. Now the very fact of seeing his poems in print helped him to recognize these more clearly and, although his mature works undoubtedly belong to the Romantics through some of their characteristics, he never again stood under Hugo's banner. Neither did many supporters of Romanticism ever forgive him for his defection. For the rest of his career he was to be haunted by critics' disappointment that later poems did not repeat the formula of the *Contes d'Espagne* and by their failure to appreciate that what he now offered them was far greater.

For almost two years Musset wrote little, but, while still living the life of a dandy, he read and thought a great deal in a period of intellectual upheaval which was probably of far greater importance for his writing than the famous emotional drama he lived through in Venice. Three events in particular had an effect on the development of his career. The first was as devastating professionally as his disappointment in love must have been emotionally. His play *La Quittance du Diable* had been accepted by the Théâtre des Nouveautés but was never performed, probably because the July Revolution interrupted the preparation of the musical score. Determined again to show his father that he could make money by his pen now that he had been allowed to give up his office post, Alfred must have been delighted when he was asked to write a play for the Odéon. Everything seemed to promise well for *La Nuit vénitienne*. The impresario was enthusiastic about it, and the actors were well cast. Yet the first night turned into the sort of chaotic shambles that must haunt playwrights in their nightmares. Whistles and shouts from the audience drowned the lines, and when the scene between the Prince and Laurette at last won the spectators' attention, the leading lady accidentally destroyed any hope of the rest of the play winning a fair hearing. Looking down from the balcony, she leaned against a trellis. The stage manager had not warned her that the paint was wet, and when she turned toward the audience again her dress was criss-crossed from waist to hem with green paint. Even without this coup de grâce, the second performance fared no better and the play was withdrawn. Almost every notice was unfavorable, and one reported such an uproar in the theater that no one except the members of the orchestra could possibly have heard the author's name, which was announced before the last curtain. Musset, still only twenty years old, was not yet the master of dramatic form which he would soon become, but the play's virtues as well as its imperfections contributed to its failure.

It was Romantic, but not with the almost melodramatic flamboyance that many of the audience must have expected from the author of the *Contes d'Espagne et d'Italie*. They were presented with character studies instead of murders, and instead of passionate rhetoric they heard a subtle, poetic dialogue to which they were unwilling to listen. Musset vowed that he would have no more to do with the "menagerie" for a long time. The two disastrous evenings had one immediately satisfactory consequence. When Musset went to thank the critic of *Le Temps* who had upbraided the audience for its behavior, he was introduced to the editor of the paper who offered him the opportunity to write a series of articles on whatever subject he chose. Without this encounter we should not have his *Revues fantastiques,* nor perhaps know what a brilliant journalist he could be.

Two other events heightened his seriousness of purpose in his career. First, at the approach of his twenty-first birthday he reviewed what he had achieved and reorganized his daily life to allow less time for his pleasures and more for study and writing; he even bought a six-month supply of tickets for the opera to have his entertainments prearranged. The next spring Alfred's father died suddenly from cholera, which had swept over much of Western Europe. The grief that struck the close-knit family was intense, and at first it seemed as if there were to be financial worries as well. Alfred's pride and sense of responsibility recoiled at the thought of being a burden on the family resources instead of helping to increase them. He vowed that he would produce a second volume of poetry, and that, if the profits did not come up to his expectations, he would give up writing as a career and enroll in one of the army's fashionable regiments.

His *Spectacle dans un fauteuil* was launched in the same way as the *Contes d'Espagne et d'Italie,* but the assembled guests listened to *La Coupe et les lèvres* and *A quoi rêvent les jeunes filles* in an icy silence, and when Musset finished reading there was none of the enthusiastic applause that had greeted *Don Paez, Portia,* and *Mardoche.* Only Mérimée showed his good judgment by coming up to praise the author, and even he seems barely to have had the courage of his convictions since Paul says that his congratulations were only murmured. When the volume was published, just before the end of 1832 but dated 1833, the press for the most part was either unfavorable or silent. Nevertheless, Sainte-Beuve stood his ground against the tide of critical opinion, quoting lines which he declared were of a quality which some poets elected to the Academy had never attained, and praising in particular the original imagery. As after the failure of *La Nuit vénitienne,* one sympathetic critic opened up for Musset a fresh opportunity. Sainte-Beuve's review had appeared in the *Revue des Deux Mondes,* whose editor now asked Musset to contribute to the periodical.

Mérimée had been right in congratulating him on the enormous progress that he had made since the *Contes d'Espagne et d'Italie. A quoi rêvent les jeunes filles* already shows what a period of intense artistic growth the two years of comparative silence had been, as Alfred worked to identify and transcribe the sound of his own individual voice. Now *André del Sarto,* published in April, 1833, was followed in the incredibly short space of six weeks by *Les Caprices de Marianne.* Although few contemporaries would recognize it, the brilliant beginner had become a master of his art. He may have told Paul shortly before he came of age that he felt his experience of life still lacked a major factor, perhaps a great love or a great grief, but it is important to remember that—in spite of his own theory that it is sorrow which forms an artist—he had shown himself a writer of genius before meeting George Sand. It is true that without his feelings for her his work would lack such poems as *Souvenir,* which is the essence of heartbreak and acceptance distilled into poetry, but it is a debatable point whether their encounter did not devastate his creative ability in the long run rather than nourish it.

IV *Venice and Its Aftermath*

The relationship which was to bring in its train both the passion and the grief that Musset suspected he lacked began in the spring of 1833. The month in which he met George Sand is usually given as June, but André Maurois presents documentary evidence that the meeting took place at the end of March or the beginning of April.[14] At a dinner given for the contributors to the *Revue des Deux Mondes,* Musset was placed next to George Sand. Without this introduction it seems unlikely that they would have sought each other out. George had already declared that Musset was too much of a dandy for her to wish to make his acquaintance, and the rather masculine figure she cut was not particularly calculated to attract him from a distance.

When they first met she was twenty-eight years old; Musset twenty-three. She lived in Paris with her two children, apart from her husband, Baron Dudevant, and she had already published two novels. From the time when Musset left Venice to the present day, torrents of ink have been poured out by writers defending or attacking her behavior toward him, and in general it is her character rather than her works which have provoked critics to verbal warfare. Some, such as André Maurois, find her on the whole an attractive and admirable personality, but to others she seems not far short of a vampire. To André Lebois she appears shrewd in business, proud, self-centered, and hard, able to change in an instant from the language of a fishwife to the exalted tones of Romantic love; above all, sexually voracious and apt to lie in wait like a fearsome spider for any prey that might fall into her power.[15] However this may be, as we try to follow her and Musset in the switchback course of their relationship, we shall see how often she looks less like an ogress than a bewildered woman, sometimes rousing our pity in her struggle to equate everyday life with Romantic ideas of love and in her very human fear of being judged in the wrong.

As far as her first impact on Musset was concerned, she had the great advantage of looking like an incarnation of some of his heroines from the *Contes d'Espagne et d'Italie.* In accordance with the idea of Spanish beauty that was the height of fashion in the Paris of that period, she had the dark brows that Musset admires in *L'Andalouse* and *Madame la Marquise,* almost hypnotic dark eyes, and the ebony hair that made the heroine of *Don Paez* look like a "young warrior-maiden with a black helmet." She herself felt that she often remained too silent a figure in the midst of glittering Parisian conversation, but under Musset's influence at their first meeting she grew animated and, unexpectedly charmed by this dandy, as they parted she invited him to visit her in her apartment.

The first maneuvers were carried out almost hesitatingly. From weekly visits, Alfred began to see George more often, and in July he wrote to her asking her to accept him, not as a lover ("The whole Baltic sea lies between you and me on that score. You can give only moral love—and I cannot give that in return to anyone"), but as a "sort of comrade of no importance and with no rights, therefore neither jealous nor quarrelsome, able to smoke your tobacco, ruffle your peignoirs, and catch colds in the head by philosophizing with you under all the chestnut trees in modern Europe" (No. XXVI). This role, not unlike that of Fantasio with Princess Elsbeth although less distant, did not satisfy Musset for long, and later in July he wrote, with the timidity that was always present beneath the dashing air he adopted, to declare that he loved her. "My dear George, I have something silly and ridiculous to say to you. Stupidly, I am writing to you instead of having spoken to you of it, I do not know why, on returning from our walk. . . . I am in love with you."

If George Sand sometimes behaved in a predatory way, she did not do so now. On the contrary, she hesitated at first to respond to his overtures. Another letter probably written during the same month implies that her reason may have been partly fear of entrusting her love to anyone of his reputation. This letter shows clearly that, if critics are right in saying that George harmed Musset mortally in Venice by convincing him that his dissolute past had made him incapable of true love, then she needed to do no more than confirm the suspicion that he himself expressed at the very outset of their affair. Here he reproaches himself with having shown her earlier only the side of himself that resembled the dissolute Octave, so that when he declared his love to her in the voice of Coelio, the shy and tender co-hero of the same play who was also a part of himself, she answered as though the former were still speaking. He heaps blame upon himself. "I can kiss a drunken, disease-ridden prostitute, but I cannot kiss my mother. . . . Love those who know how to love, I know only how to suffer" (No. XXIX).

When she relented, this somber mood must soon have been forgotten in weeks which had moments of carefree gaiety. George, writing to Sainte-Beuve in August, confessed that she was deeply in love with Musset, and according to *Elle et lui,* her account of their life together, his moods of madcap exuberance made her feel ten years younger. Now the debauchee Octave had given way to the Fantasio who whisked the Prince of Mantua's wig off his head on the end of a fishing line. One glimpse through the windows of the apartment on the Quai Malaquais shows us a dinner party from which Musset seemed to be missing. The guests were waited on at table by a golden-haired, blue-eyed maid, bare-armed, short-skirted, and with a cross around her neck, a maid who ended the meal in unorthodox fashion by emptying a jugful of water over the head of a grave philosopher, Lerminier.

To the observer, a century later, these halcyon weeks seem to have been the happiest in a life that was to grow more and more dismal. Musset had known gaiety before, but now his wit bubbled up from the happiness of the mutual love which was perhaps his greatest expectation in life. Jean Pommier believes that the lovers' stay in Fontainebleau took place as early as August, rather than in September, as is usually said;[16] in any case with this visit came the first recorded cloud in their sky. By Romantic standards, these days should have been idyllic. The lovers would walk in the forest at night, as Octave and Brigitte do in the *Confession.* One night, after a trivial quarrel, Alfred fell victim to one of those hallucinations which had visited him since childhood. This time the hallucination was aural as well as visual. He heard what seemed to be an echo singing a snatch of an obscene song and then saw himself, older, ragged, and with a ravaged face, running through the undergrowth. What happened exactly is not known; later accounts vary according to which side commentators took in the Sand-Musset arguments, but it seems certain that George was as terrified by this transformation of her witty, elegant lover into a seemingly near-crazed being as Alfred was terrified by his vision.

On their return to Paris the optimistic gaiety of earlier days seems to have escaped them. Before they met, George had been planning a stay in Italy. Now she announced her intention of setting off alone, and against the accusation of the harm she did Musset in Venice must be set the fact that, far from luring him there, she had to be persuaded at first that he should accompany her. The next obstacle was the reluctance of Musset's mother to see her son set off on such a journey. When Alfred broached the subject, her tears made him decide to abandon his plans; but that same evening, according to Paul, when Madame de Musset was sitting at the fireside with her daughter, a message came that a lady was waiting outside in a carriage and asking to speak to her. It seems that George vowed to look after Alfred with all the care that a mother could show and that her assurances won the day.

It is true that the maternal side of George's character was strongly developed, but she can hardly have looked a motherly figure as she appeared in pearl-gray trousers and a tasseled cap to board the coach for Lyons. Paul, who saw the couple off, tells of so many ill omens attending the coach's departure that, as Maurice Donnay points out, any self-respecting ancient Roman would have decided the journey was to be ill-fated and would have abandoned it. In fact, all went well, and the boat journey down the Rhône from Lyons to Avignon was enlivened by Stendhal's quips. During the sea passage from Marseilles to Genoa Alfred suffered the humiliation of being seasick just as Chopin did when he traveled with George to Mallorca, a humiliation which must have been intensified by seeing George in the best of health, calmly smoking a cigarette. After visiting Genoa, they traveled to Florence, the city that Musset brings vividly to life in *Lorenzaccio,* and from there went on to Venice early in January, 1834.

Now the story took a turn only too familiar in common experience. The stay abroad which had seemed so idyllic a prospect began to prove quite the reverse in reality. In the apartment on the Quai Malaquais, their familiar city around them and their circle of friends had cushioned them to some extent against the clash of their temperaments, but now in a hotel room in unknown surroundings they were forced into each other's company almost exclusively. This might have been ideal if their tastes and habits had dovetailed, but they were at the same time too similar and too dissimilar for life together to be tolerable. Nor were events kind to them. George fell ill with fever and dysentery and had to stay in bed for a fortnight. A young man of twenty-four, impatient to explore the fascinating foreign town which lies outside his window, does not necessarily make a good nurse, and it seems that Alfred became bored at being confined in their room at the Albergo Danieli near the Grand Canal, and even perhaps slightly petulant that anyone should waste time by falling ill on a holiday. Some biographers suggest that it was partly to hide his distaste at George's illness that he began to spend more and more time away from her; at all events his boredom and loneliness caused him to fall back into the dissolute ways which were repugnant to her. She, lonely too, would hear him returning in the early hours of the morning, once with his clothes torn and his face bloodstained, sometimes ready to pick a quarrel with her, much as Octave does with Brigitte in the *Confession.*

Before he himself fell ill, the affair was over already as far as George was concerned. Exasperated by her frigidity and her sermonizing, Alfred declared one day that he no longer loved her, and she replied that the feeling was mutual. To someone of Musset's quicksilver moods this meant nothing. In later years his housekeeper was so well aware of his stormy changefulness that on the many occasions when he dismissed her she would simply pack her bags and leave by the front door only to slip in again at the back and wait for his mood to pass. To George, however, this mutual rejection was as final as a legal divorce. She now considered herself free. When Musset became dangerously ill with the malarial fever which contributed to the heart complaint that finally killed him, she nursed him devotedly, but she saw no moral grounds why she should not fall in love with the handsome young Dr. Pagello whom she called in. Biographer after biographer has discussed the dramatic events which took place in Musset's hotel room, so dramatic that it is strange that no British or American film maker has given his version of the story.

Each incident in the changing relationship between George and the doctor has been debated in detail. The testimony of three people who might have spoken authoritatively is of limited value, for Pagello did not write his account until many years later, George was bent on protecting her reputation, and Musset swung at this time between lucidity and bouts of delirium when he shouted, sang, and once ran naked about the room in spite of the attempts of two men to put him back to bed.

It seems to have been George this time who made the advances, handing to Pagello a sheet of impassioned questions and declarations. The most hotly debated problem has been whether or not they were actually lovers while Musset still lay ill. The invalid himself had imprinted on his memory a picture of George sitting on Pagello's knee, kissing him; he remembered too seeing a single cup from which they must both have drunk. But the sickbed recollections of a man intermittently raving with brain fever were bound to be suspect, especially when his nurse wished to throw doubt upon them. Even if the findings of the literary private-detective work that has been carried out were conclusive, surely what must have mattered most to Musset—again in love with the George who had tended him with such solicitude—were the feelings which she and Pagello had for each other rather than whether they had yet given physical expression to those feelings.

The evidence seems to indicate that she was in fact already Pagello's mistress before Musset recovered, but, since she no longer considered herself bound to her former lover, probably her real fault lay in the way in which she threatened him and managed to persuade him that it was he who was to blame for everything that had happened. Even this is understandable when one realizes how afraid she must have been, both for her reputation in France and for her actual physical safety since Musset, in his understandably violent first reaction, seems to have threatened to kill both her and Pagello. Late one night, seeing a light under her door, Musset went into George's room and found her in bed writing a letter which she tried to hide from him. When he guessed that it was for Pagello, she grew angry and warned him that she would have him committed to an asylum if he did not leave her alone. To someone newly recovered from brain fever, the idea that he might actually have crossed the border into insanity for a time was devastating. Musset, back in his own room, heard George open the window and guessed that she was throwing out her torn-up letter.

At dawn the next day he found her, in her petticoat and a shawl, searching the street for the fragments. Again she threatened him with the madhouse and ran off, with Musset in pursuit. The chase, with the distraught couple moving against the background of Venice, sounds like an excerpt from a film scenario. George threw herself into a gondola, but Alfred leaped in after her. In silence they reached the Lido, and George took to her heels again, jumping from tomb to tomb in the Jews' cemetery, so Maurice Donnay tells us.[17] At last she collapsed on a tombstone. Alfred wrung from her the confession that she loved the doctor and took her back to the hotel.

In her first moments of fear, casting around for any weapon, one can understand how George could stoop to terrifying Musset with the suggestion of madness. It is far less easy to stomach the fact that later she could dress the same idea up in highfalutin language and publish it in cold blood in the first of the *Lettres d'un voyageur* (May 1, 1834). "God," she writes, "angered by your rebellion and your pride, laid a hand burning with wrath upon your brow and, in an instant, your thoughts grew confused, your reason left you." As though it were not enough to suffer from malaria, Alfred was burdened with the idea that his illness was his own fault. For the rest of his life he was haunted by the fear that he might be committed to an asylum by someone who misunderstood his nervous attacks, and his housekeeper's memoirs show that this fear played at least some part in his reluctance to take a wife.

He was made to feel that he alone was responsible for his emotional as well as for his physical suffering. Frightened no doubt by his thoughts of vengeance, George harped on the idea that Alfred himself had destroyed their relationship because his debauchery had made him incapable of real love. Soon he saw himself as the guilty instead of the injured party in the trio; George, instead of a faithless mistress, as the essence of ill-treated virtue; and Pagello as the noble soul who had cared for him in his illness and comforted George in her distress. It would be unfair to imply that George invented the belief that Musset's capacity for love was already irrevocably destroyed by his taste for wine and women. As we saw, he was already afraid at the outset of the affair that something like this might happen. Her guilt lay in convincing him that the events of their Italian journey were a practical demonstration that he was unfit for a relationship based on deep and lasting feelings. Ever afterwards the specter of these events seems to have helped to blight with self-doubt Musset's attempts at finding lasting happiness with a woman, and since for him love was the most powerful inspiration for writing, the accusation that George had a share in murdering him intellectually may not be far from the truth.

Still convinced that he was an unworthy part of a trio whose other two members were virtuous and generous, Alfred set off for Paris, leaving the new lovers in peace. Paul and his mother had been so anxious after not hearing from him for six weeks that they were about to leave for Italy. They were scarcely reassured when the long-awaited letter warned them that Alfred was on his way back with "an ailing body, a crushed spirit, a mangled heart . . . ," and indeed the time that lay between his return to France and the final rupture with George in 1835 was probably one of even greater anguish for him than the catastrophic days through which he had lived in Venice. Periods of great stress often seem to bring with them a slight feeling of unreality which acts as a partial analgesic. Now Musset was left with long days full of physical weakness and the awareness of his loss. Paul's biography gives a toned-down account of his convalescence; Alfred's own letters strike the reader, to my mind, with such an impact of suffering and struggling against that suffering that sometimes, like scenes from *Romeo and Juliet,* they are almost unbearable in their intensity.

Nor do they form a mere literary weeping wall, as one might have feared. Critics often speak of Musset's weakness of character, but many of these pages are dignified by attempts to surmount his despair. On April 19 he tells George that he has hurled himself back into his old life in society despite the slow fever that returns every evening, and at the end of the month he writes: "And yet I shall have other mistresses; now the trees are growing green and the scent of the lilacs wafts in; everything is coming to life again and my heart leaps in spite of myself" (No. XXXVII. April 30). Yet in this same letter he tells that he has taken from her empty apartment a broken comb which he carries everywhere with him, and soon he had to admit that the pleasures of his old life would not serve as an escape for him. He was fighting a losing battle against depression. "God is a witness to my struggles . . . they say that time heals everything. I was a hundred times stronger the day I came home than I am now. Everything is crumbling around me. When I have spent the morning weeping, kissing your portrait, saying such idiotic things to your ghost that they make me shudder, I take my hat, I wander here and there. . . ." (No. XXXVIII). In the same letter he talks of blotting out his troubles (it is not clear to me whether he means by suicide or by rum and opium) but once again "The Spring will not allow it; the flowers and all this greenery call me back to life." His nerves are so on edge that he dare not risk finding relief with a prostitute for fear of strangling her, a fear that is justified by stories of his violent behavior on some such occasions.

Where one would expect self-pity there is self-reproach for his supposed failure to love George as she deserved and a touchingly sincere concern for her well-being, especially when he hears that she does not have enough money for food and again when she mentions suicide (Nos. XL and XLI). In July he even manages to write a friendly, witty letter to Pagello (No. XLIII), but the theme that clamors through this long series of letters is his passionate love for George, expressed so simply and yet so overwhelmingly that it is strange she did not take the coach for Paris much sooner, and without Pagello.

One letter, written to George after she and Pagello had reached Paris and Musset had had a devastating interview with her, expresses love with an almost Cornelian ring. "Although you have known me as a child, you must realize that I am a man now. . . . It may well be that I am in despair; but it is not despair that governs my actions, it is I who take stock of it, calculate its strength, and control it. . . . I am experiencing the only love of my life. . . . I know that it is invincible but that, however invincible it may be, my will shall be a match for it" (No. XLVI. Undated). By September he was in Baden, trying to ease his unhappiness with the ancient remedy of travel, and finding instead that his feelings reached a new paroxysm. The frenzied letter he wrote to George is all the more painful to read because of its contrast with his earlier attempts at control and because, to my mind, there is not a trace of Romantic posing in it.

It is a week now since I left, and I have not written to you yet. I was waiting for a moment of calm; there are none now. . . . I wanted to speak to you only of my love; ah! George, what love! No man has ever loved as I love you. I am lost, you see; I am drowned in love, overwhelmed by it; I no longer know whether I live, eat, walk, breathe, or talk; I know that I love. . . . I love you, my flesh and my blood! I am dying of love, an endless, indescribable love without a name, crazy, desperate, lost! . . . No! I shall not be cured. No, I shall not try to live; and I prefer it this way; to die loving you is better than life. . . . (No. XLIX. September 1)

Before any Anglo-Saxon makes fun of such an outburst he should at least consider whether in his early twenties he never experienced feelings approaching these, even though he would not have dreamed of expressing them in these terms.

Pagello soon returned to Italy, his role as George's lover at an end, and Alfred's letters during the autumn of 1834 reflect a pattern of rhapsodic reunions with George, inevitably followed by shattering quarrels and remorse, attempts to part, and the passionate longing for each other which would bring them together again, restarting the cycle. Their friends—Sainte-Beuve, Tattet, and Boucoiran—tried to wrench apart the partners in this dance of death, and both lovers struggled to escape. One November day Alfred left George standing on his doorstep, refusing to allow her into the house, but in March, 1835, when she finally tore herself away and fled to her home in the country, he immediately wrote to the friend who had helped her leave, asking her whereabouts (No. LXIX. Undated).

For some time now George had been as passionately in love with Alfred as he was with her. Her outburst in her *Journal intime* is far more rhetorical than Musset's descriptions of his feelings, but it too seems heavy with a load of real grief. Book after book, from Musset's self-accusing *Confession* and George's *Elle et lui* onwards, has retraced their story and tried to apportion the blame for its disastrous nature. As far as physical appearance was concerned, each came close to the other's ideal, but one of the most interesting analyses by Gastinel shows how, temperamentally, they were at the same time too alike and too different to find life together bearable. It would probably not have mattered that their political inclinations diverged, but so too did almost all their tastes. He loved town life and she the country; he preferred poetry, she prose; she enjoyed discussing literature, while he was reluctant to do so; he had a sense of the ridiculous and she had little; she moralized endlessly, and he found sermonizing intolerable.

This last factor must have played a large part in ruining the early days of their stay in Italy, for George did not realize that, while Alfred was spending his days in a totally different way from her solid eight hours of pen-pushing at her desk, he too was putting the time to the best possible use for his writing. Her method was to pour out a steady flow of pages each day (never stopping to plan or to cross out, complained Alfred) with a regularity which made her critics declare that she had an ink well where her heart should be, or call her "une vache à l'encre." To her, routine seemed essential for financial security, and she continually took Musset to task when he spent his days roaming round the town, exploring Italian streets and squares, jotting down an impression in the notebook which accompanied him everywhere, or making a sketch in his album, settling himself at a café table if an idea or a scene needed developing at any length. This totally opposed way of following the same profession, George putting her faith in routine and Musset in inspiration, illustrates the strange combination of affinities and contrasts that they present. As far as similarities are concerned, Charles Maurras points out that both had the same qualities which are usually labeled typically masculine and feminine.[18] Both had the strength of intellect and personality which are commonly described as masculine; both had the same intense sensitivity and the capriciousness which are said to be feminine characteristics. If either had possessed these traits in a different degree, their characters might have harmonized; as it was, they clashed continually.

As far as love was concerned, both were bedeviled by the Romantic tendency to be in love with love itself, trying to realize skyscraping ideals of both physical pleasure and communion of soul, and both had past failures to attain this ideal stored in their memories. They were no better matched sexually than temperamentally. George's dark gaze, which men thought so passionate, seemed to promise an ardor which she did not really possess. Musset refers in his letters to her failure to give him great pleasure, and so too does Dr. Odinot in describing their encounter as that "d'une anaphrodisie et d'une névrose épileptiforme" *(Etude médico-psychologique sur Alfred de Musset,* quoted by Gastinel, pp. 362-63).

V *The Post-Venice Years*

Most people with an affection for French literature know of Musset's brilliant and precocious debut in literary society and of the hectic tragedy of his love for George Sand. Comparatively few pay as much attention to his life after 1835, and the tendency is to look on this time as no more than a coda to the dazzling years of his youth. Even some of his contemporaries regarded him when his thirtieth birthday was past as a ghost who continued to move among them. They pointed to his decreasing rate of publication, to days apparently squandered on alcohol and prostitutes, to a life consumed, some imagined, by continuing grief for the failure of his relationship with George or at least by the sheer emptiness the end of the affair left in him. Yet these years seem to me the most fascinating of all, although toward the end they convey to those who study them something of the terrible desolation of a life often lived close to despair. From the creative point of view, the post-Venice years certainly did not constitute a uniform desert. As we said, Musset had worked out his own literary manner and beliefs before his encounter with George, and for some years after they had parted his poetry and plays continued to appear, fashioned in the same mold but now with the greater intensity which was due to his experiences of passion and suffering. His taste in both art and literature moved more and more toward Classical simplicity and stylized beauty, a taste symbolized in 1839 by his affair with Rachel, the actress who helped to revive enthusiasm for Racine. It was only during the last three years or so of his life that his writings dwindled almost to nothing.

As far as events of any magnitude are concerned, there is little after the Italian adventure for the biographer to tell, and from 1835 on it is particularly true that nearly everything of significance in Musset's life took place in the secret theater of his mind. The outside world saw him take up his life with the elegant set of dandies, spending afternoons at the Club de Natation, going from there to the Café de Paris and then to some salon or other entertainment. This cycle was interrupted regularly by periods when lack of funds and the consequent need to work to replenish his purse kept him at home. "When some lines by M. Musset appear somewhere, one can be sure that M. Musset is also going to appear. If M. Musset comes into circulation first, his poem will not be slow to follow" (J. Lecomte, "Lettres de Van Engelgom," *Indépendance belge*, 1837, quoted by Gastinel, p. 519). In 1838 his life became a little easier financially when he was appointed librarian at the Ministry of the Interior.

Musset had looked on his twenty-first birthday seriously, as an important milestone in his life. In his thirtieth year he again reviewed his life and career, and found them sadly wanting. His health did not encourage him to take an optimistic outlook, for early in 1840 he fell gravely ill and fresh strain was put on his heart, already damaged by the fever he had contracted in Venice. His mother and sister despaired of controlling their obstreperous patient until a nun, Sister Marcelline, quelled and soothed him with her gentle authority, winning his lasting affection. Convalescence was not easy for Musset. From this time on the state of his health clearly advised that he should moderate his hectic search for pleasure or for momentary forgetfulness in drink and womanizing. Yet this illness had left him in a dreary state of lassitude, and when he tried to impose a sober routine on his days, he fell victim to a neurasthenia as harmful as his excesses. Frantically trying to rediscover some of the champagne sparkle of life which had made existence seem worth while, he hurled himself again into the dandies' round of gaiety. One night when a group of friends was staying at Alfred Tattet's house at Bury and had spent an apparently cheerful evening together, Musset's room was found empty, and on the table lay a sonnet which was a sad commentary on his efforts to recapture the others' high spirits: "I have lost my strength and my life and my friends and my gaiety; I have lost even the pride which made me believe in my genius" *(Tristesse*, 1840). The lines rang out with the heaviness of a knell, completely different in mood from the sonnet celebrating the joys of life which Musset had written two years earlier during another stay with Tattet, this time at his estate on the edge of the forest of Montmorency.

The first quatrain of *Tristesse* spoke of disillusionment with his career, and Musset began to suffer more intensely than before from the double load of feeling that the public—except perhaps the young—misjudged and underrated his work, and that he himself had never given adequate expression to what he had to say. "Have no doubt of it, this fleeting spark contained in my skull is something divine. . . . As yet I have heard no more than the first notes of the melody which is perhaps within me. I have managed to do no more than tune this instrument which will soon crumble into dust, but what delight it has given me" *(Le Poète déchu*, IV).

A writer who was interested mainly in form, in combining words to reproduce the mosaic of his dreams, might have found his work a refuge from his disappointments, but for Musset writing was the afterglow of emotions which life used to afford him, and now rarely provided. Nor was he the sort of man who could dull the edge of his disillusion with the commonplace pleasures of everyday existence, with hot buttered toast and slippers warmed before the fire. "Je n'ai jamais été *banal,*" he once wrote, adding that the petty, restricted life which most people led destroyed their potentialities (No. CVIII. September, 1840). All that remained for him was to try to reduce his depression to manageable proportions each day by the amount of alcohol or drugs which he prescribed for himself. From 1840 onwards illness after illness weakened him, increasing his dejection, and the amazing thing is the degree of control which he seems to have exercised over the "orgies" that made some contemporaries describe him as a monster. Contrary to some impressions, he did not allow himself to slide downhill in a roistering, drunken stupor, surrounded by prostitutes. During the last seventeen years or so of his life, he would appear at the Café de la Régence every evening like an automaton at eight o'clock and sit, usually alone, drinking a mixture of absinthe and Strasbourg beer until midnight. Often his cigar ash would fall into his glass, but his thought was so little on his drink that he would absent-mindedly swallow the mixture. Like some somber Cinderella, he would rise from his table at midnight and make a usually dignified exit, rarely needing any help to reach the door.

There are stories of his being noisily drunk, but it seems to have been exceptional for him to lose control over himself. Far from giving him pleasure, his dependence on alcohol and on the prostitutes, who, incongruously enough, were the guests at his celebration supper party when *Carmosine* was accepted for publication, was yet another cause for self-disgust. Yet these opiates were essential if he were to continue living at all. Their function was merely that of the drugs which a twentieth-century doctor would have prescribed to alleviate his depressive illness. Once Madame Jaubert remonstrated with him over his addiction to alcohol, but his explanation of his need for it was so convincing and so tragic that she was filled with remorse for having chided him.

At last the Academy elected him a member in 1852, but it had already injured his pride on three occasions, twice by failing to elect him and once by offering him the insult of a literary prize intended to encourage a promising beginner. (Musset reacted with both tact and hauteur, accepting the prize money but donating it to a charitable fund.) At last too the theater made some reparation for *La Nuit vénitienne* by successfully putting on *Un Caprice* in 1847. How could it have happened, demanded Gautier, that the actors had not long ago begged the author on bended knee to give them plays as subtle, witty, and poetic as this?[19] Yet the dramatic critics were not always kind to Musset in these later years of his life. It is not altogether surprising to hear one journalist declaring in 1849 that *Louison* proved Musset to be already dead and describing it as September rain in comparison with the April sunshine of his earlier plays, but it is strange to find so many critics failing to appreciate the adaptations of earlier works when they were at last staged.

Meanwhile the circle of Musset's family and of his few intimate friends lost some of its links, depressing him still more. Alfred Tattet left Paris to live in the country, and in 1846 Musset's sister married and was soon joined by her mother in Angers. Now it was the housekeeper chosen by Madame de Musset who took over the task of easing life for him and keeping at bay his terrible hallucinations. There are several stories about Musset's uncanny perceptiveness, and one anecdote told by the housekeeper, Adèle Colin, illustrates both this and the nature of his nightmare visions. When a neighbor died, she did not tell her master for fear of troubling him. At two o'clock in the morning she was woken by a frantic ringing of his bedside bell. "Stand there," he begged her in terror, pointing to the foot of his bed, "where the undertaker is; he says he's waiting for me, he's wrapped in a black sheet; as soon as you stop talking, he reappears."[20]

All the years from 1835 to his death in 1857, which have few events or changes of fortune as demarcation lines, could be related in terms of the long line of women who figured in his life. Prostitutes, working girls, actresses, society women, at least one princess—their story is a fascinating one and well worth reading in Léon Séché's biography. No doubt many of them meant no more to Musset than his absinthe and beer; others at the end of his life were young girls whose platonic hero worship he accepted, in much the same spirit as the king in *Carmosine*. With those whom he loved deeply for a time—the blonde Aimée d'Alton who brought him happiness until he tired of her, and who later married his brother; the glacial Princess Belgiojoso, as dark-eyed as George Sand; Madame Allan-Despréaux, the actress mainly responsible for the staging of *Un Caprice*—he was seeking not just passion but a lasting companionship, "an affection which habit and old age would have turned into something very dear, without even sleeping exactly together, but just under the same roof" (quoted by Séché, vol. II, p. 92).

Thanks to Madame Allan-Despréaux's letters, her experiences as Musset's mistress are almost as well documented as are George Sand's, and they show how much George and many other women must have had to suffer from him. The couple had rented the sculptor Pradier's house in the country at Ville-d'Avray, and some of their time there was idyllic. At other times there would be violent quarrels, caused by the jealousy which sprang up in Musset for no reason, a cynical jealousy whose roots were to some extent in his libertine past. Occasionally he would disappear for three or four days, leaving no idea of his whereabouts. In a well-known passage, Madame Allan describes the lover who was sometimes ideal, sometimes almost demonic:

I have never seen a more striking contrast than the two beings contained in this one person. One is good, gentle, tender, enthusiastic, full of wit and common sense, naïve (this is an extraordinary thing), as naïve as a child, good-natured, simple, unpretentious, modest, sensitive, idealistic, weeping over the slightest thing which comes from the heart, an exquisite artist in every sphere, feeling and expressing everything beautiful in the most beautiful language—music, painting, literature, the drama. If you turn the page and look on the other side, you find a man possessed by a sort of devil, weak, violent, proud, tyrannical, crazy, hard, small-minded, insultingly distrustful, blindly obstinate, as self-centered and egotistical as it is possible to be, blaspheming everything, and throwing himself as wholeheartedly into evil as he does into good. . . . His nature consists of extremes, both good and bad. When the latter is uppermost, nothing can halt it except a bout of illness, which has the effect of restoring his reason. . . . I cannot imagine how he has managed to survive so long, and why he has not died on a thousand occasions. (Quoted by Séché, vol. II, pp. 193-94).

Beyond the ravaged profligate that the public saw, and even beyond the Jekyll and Hyde figure that his mistresses knew, Musset's own letters take us closest to him—to his charm and wit, his good sense and artistic integrity, his despair and weariness. Often the recipient of his letters was Madame Jaubert, a former mistress who, after Musset's jealousy had ended their affair, remained a lifelong friend. Many lines he wrote to her show the same fantasy as some of the *Comédies et Proverbes,* as when he addressed a mock legalistic letter to "madame Jaubert, domiciled in the street where your house is, aged as many spring-times as next year's lilacs, tiny in size and wholesome in mind" (No. CXXVII. November 21, 1842), declared that "cheese-mites are the happiest of all creatures: they live only one day and they spend it waltzing" (No. LXXV. August 11, 1835), or wrote that "The great thing in life is conscientiously to talk nonsense. When one no longer dares to talk nonsense, one must blow one's brains out or get married" (No. XCIX. 1839).

Every now and again the lightness of tone gives way to somberness. In 1836 he wrote that he was beginning to feel "absolutely disgusted that all-night sessions, which my head and my chest forbid me, cannot rescue me from a past which is crushing me physically and morally" (LXXIX. April 1, 1836). Four years later he assured the Duchesse de Castries that faith in God was inborn in him, although he knew himself to be immature in religious matters; the cause of his melancholy was that the love affair of which he was cured had left him "dried up, like a fish in the middle of a cornfield; I never could, nor can I now or in the future, live alone like this, nor even feel that this *is* living" (No. CVIII. September, 1840). At times he felt weary even of complaining: "if I lose this resource, there will be nothing left to do but to throw flowers on my tomb" (No. CXX. July 26, 1842).

Only rarely does he allow his depression to appear without masking it in flippancy, but when in all seriousness he explains his experience of life to Aimée d'Alton his analysis is striking in its perception and its sense of proportion. Others may have tried to make Musset's life seem a melodrama of passion and debauchery, but he did not:

I am a year older than you in age, and ten in experience. Do not smile at this word "experience," my experience does not amount to much; let me tell you what it has taught me. To have splendid dreams and try to make them real is the first and inevitable condition of great hearts. Yet when we make our entrance into life, reality and its countless disappointments are bound sooner or later to strike a blow at virgin hopes and knock them to the ground when they are flying at their highest. . . . The first experience, Aimée, lies in suffering, in discovering and realizing that *absolute* dreams are scarcely ever attainable. . . . A feeling of bitter reflectiveness, therefore, is the result of this first trial. The heart, hurt to the very quick in its first rush of enthusiasm, bleeds and seems incurably torn. Yet one goes on living, and one must love to stay alive; one loves fearfully, distrustfully, and gradually a man looks around and realizes that life is not as sad as it seemed; he comes to himself again, comes back to happiness, to God and to the truth.[21]

Later letters to Aimé show how his nervous condition would never allow him to enjoy for long the eminently sensible outlook he had described. In January, 1838, he told her how he had been in an unbearable state for a week, tortured by remorse because he thought his misery was his own fault, dropping with weariness, and longing to escape from himself for a few hours. When Aimée offered to marry him, he declared that it would be a crime to involve her more closely with him, and later he described in phrases dragging with weariness his feeling of utter emotional emptiness: "It is not grief, nor anger, nor even boredom; my heart is fading away, life is no longer either dear or hateful to me; it is pointless, indifferent. . . . I am giving up the struggle, I cannot keep it up. My fate is settled, it was settled long ago by me myself."[22] If only George Sand and his own ideals had not harped on his indulgence in wine and women—tastes which many an eminent and respectable man has shared and then conveniently forgotten—he could perhaps have been spared some of the load of self-reproach by seeing how even in childhood his nervous disposition promised no easy life.

One of his last letters to Adèle Colin is pitiful in the depth of physical and mental misery it reveals. "I have not shut my eyes, the first attacks of my delirium have started; you are the only one who can cope with them, come, I cannot manage without you" (No. CLXIV. 1849). Yet his last days had their highlights, including the evening when he was allowed to wander alone among his beloved pictures in the Louvre. Music too had always had the power to charm and soothe him, and the sound of his sister playing his favorite piano pieces would coax him out of his room even in his blackest moods.

The condition of his heart worsened rapidly during the winter of 1856. Steadfastly refusing to pay any attention to his health unless he was prostrate in bed, he had at least agreed from the summer of 1854 onwards to tear himself away from Paris during the hottest months, exchanging the sultriness of the city for the fresher air of the coast, first at Le Croisic and during the last two years of his life at Le Havre. In March, 1857, unable to find a carriage to take him to the Academy to vote for Emile Augier, he insisted on setting out on foot through pouring rain, although he was so ill that he had to stop every few yards to recover his breath. His vote tipped the balance in Augier's favor and, under the tonic effect of the excitement, Musset rounded off the evening by dining out and going to the theater. "Do not be angry," he urged his housekeeper on his return. "This may be the last time; my friend Tattet is calling me [he had died recently], and I think that I shall soon be going to join him."

In fact he was to appear just once more in Parisian society, at a dinner given by Prince Napoleon at the Palais-Royal. It is pleasant to think that not only was the occasion a glittering one, but that Musset himself was at his dazzling best as a conversationalist. His condition had made dressing such a lengthy affair that he had arrived when the guests were at table and, to compensate his host for this, he summoned all his wit and intelligence to add to the enjoyment of the evening. Returning home exhausted, he went to bed and was never again able to leave it. On April 26 Paul was summoned from Angers, and to him we owe an eye-witness account of the peaceful ending of a life which had rarely known peace. When he arrived he found Alfred in bed, suffering from time to time from one of his usual fainting fits, but feeling no discomfort in the intervals, content to chat or have someone read to him.

On May 1, his doctor felt that a specialist should be called in, but both physicians judged that Musset's life was in no immediate danger. Paul tells that the day was untroubled and that, having for once been a model patient, Alfred felt considerably better toward evening. "What a splendid thing peace is!" he is reported to have said. "People are certainly wrong to be afraid of death which is no more than its highest expression." He was in a cheerful frame of mind, making plans for the future, and spent much of the evening talking affectionately of all those who were dear to him, among them Sister Marcelline. The two brothers talked quietly until one o'clock the next morning, when Alfred suddenly sat bolt upright with an expression of mingled surprise and attentiveness, and put his hand to his heart. When Paul asked if he was in pain, he shook his head. To other questions he made no reply except to lay his head back on the pillow and say as he shut his eyes: "Sleep! At last I am going to sleep!" He died shortly afterwards without regaining consciousness.

VI *L'Enfant du Siècle*

Few biographies tempt the reader more than Musset's to play the no-doubt highly unacademic game of supposing "If only . . ." If only he had met Aimée d'Alton before George Sand, or if only the Parisian theater had provided him earlier with an interest in life and some satisfaction for his professional pride, might he then have found existence bearable? One of the most intricate of these blind alleys lies in imagining Musset in a different period and guessing whether he might have fared better in an age which preached reason and self-mastery rather than passion, or which held firmer beliefs about the purpose of life. Certainly Musset himself was convinced that the period in which he lived had had a blighting effect on his generation, an argument to which he devotes the whole of the much-quoted second chapter of the

Confession. During the Napoleonic Wars, he writes, women anxious for the safety of soldier-husbands and sons had given birth to a generation which was intense, pale, highly strung (the usual figure cut by Romantics in life and in literature). He describes how boys at this time grew up in schools run on military lines, where boyish dreams, such as Alfred de Vigny's, centered on heroism in battle, on conquering an empire for France. In this hectic atmosphere even death itself seemed glamorous.

Then came the shock of disillusion and purposelessness when France, far from building an empire, was left exhausted and ruined. Royalty, the Church, and political ideals were discredited; "all human illusions, like trees in autumn, shed their leaves around them." The would-be heroes were left in a no-man's-land of boredom and aimlessness, stranded between the ruins of France as it had been and a future which was still unshaped. Even social life and fashions grew dreary under English influence, the chapter continues, and love itself was treated with scorn. Goethe and Byron contributed to the atmosphere of cynicism in which idealists gave themselves up to despair and everyone else to amassing money. It is small wonder that the young flung themselves into debauchery in an attempt to escape from this devastating emotional and spiritual vacuum. More positively, literature stormed the Bastille of Classical doctrines and made an assault on the senses of its public with vivid visual effects and violent emotions. After universality, the individual was now paramount, intent on the vibration of his own nerve endings. There was nothing here to help free Musset from the tyranny of his temperament; there was only encouragement for him to abandon himself to it.

"The incarnation of springtime," "corruption itself," "a peach on a bed of nettles"—Musset provoked extreme and sometimes contradictory comments from his contemporaries. To Paul, Alfred was mirrored in Fantasio, and Fantasio comes close to being an enigma. To a twentieth-century psychologist, skilled in understanding those emotional and nervous disabilities which Musset complained met no sympathy—although they were as real as broken limbs—his personality would surely seem less contradictory and certainly less reprehensible than it did to some of those who surrounded him. His life is chiefly remembered for its brilliant literary debut and for the love story which had most of the elements of a Romantic drama, but to me it seems more fascinating and touching in its clear-sighted struggle to find anyone or anything that could make life seem worth living. A vainer man would have found the necessary satisfaction in pride in his gifts; a more materialistic one in turning to the more profitable forms of writing; Musset's very qualities, as well as his failings, left him virtually defenseless in a fight already prejudiced by his nervous constitution. If his story had merely been that of the archetypal Romantic hero, desolate in love, it would justifiably seem out of date now. In its preoccupation with the gulf between dreams and reality, with finding a purpose and a moving force for life, it makes Musset "le plus *nous tous*" not only for the Romantic age but for any time.

CHAPTER 2

"Le Poète déchu."
Narrative Works in Prose

*"Le prosateur ... a une affaire
pressée, c'est de dire ce qu'il pense et
non autre chose." (Le Poète déchu,*
Fragment VIII)

I *Musset's Attitude Toward Short-Story Writing*

SUDDENLY faced with the task of supporting his family on the
money he can earn by his pen, the hero of Musset's fragmentary
novel from which the title of this chapter is borrowed tells how he went
to see a publisher with the proposal that he should write some poetry.
There was little demand for this type of commodity at the moment, the
market was bad, replied the publisher, but he was willing to pay twenty
sous a copy if the disappointed poet cared to write a novel *(Le Poète
déchu,* fragment VI). In the last section of this work, Musset maintains
that he has no wish to disparage prose in comparison with poetry by
claiming that one is pedestrian while the other has wings, but
nevertheless the incident between the poet and the publisher probably
illustrates his own association of prose with the mundane world of
financial necessity. Perhaps he was limiting prose here to that of the
novel and the short story; his own dramatic prose is no more
earthbound than his poetry.

Certainly it seems to be Musset speaking personally when the
thwarted poet describes how he chafed under the burden of producing
a set number of pages a day with a deadline continually threatening
him, a burden made all the heavier because, whether through ignorance,
natural aversion, or laziness as a writer, he loathed prose (VI). To
Musset, who preferred to write when the inclination took him, in a
room filled with flowers to welcome his muse, such humdrum
hackwork must have been anathema. Small wonder that one day,
counting the manuscript pages of *Croisilles* and calculating the amount
of space the story would take up in the *Revue des Deux Mondes,* he
cried "Finis prosae" and refused to lengthen the abrupt ending by one
word.

[37]

The final fragment of *Le Poète déchu* provides some of the reasons for this forsaking of prose for poetry. The strength of prose lies in reflection, Musset says. Poetry, on the other hand, scarcely ever consists of this type of material but is in fact the fruit of even deeper thought. The poet must seize the crux of an idea, and yet manage to concentrate in a short space at least a suggestion of a multitude of corollaries upon which the reader can meditate at his will. As for musical quality, melody is the essence of poetry but the prose writer runs the risk of weakening the force of his ideas if he pays too much attention to style. Prose may show taste by an avoidance of dissonance and by a harmonious grouping of words, but it has no set rhythm and can have no melody. It follows that the author who tried to make his prose melodious would be wasting time in as pointless a fashion as a man on urgent business who insisted on progressing down the street in a series of complicated dance steps instead of walking straight ahead. In Musset's view, then, prose and poetry are an entirely different species, almost hostile to each other, and an awareness of these opinions and feelings makes several characteristics of style and technique easier to understand as we open the *Nouvelles,* the *Contes,* and the various other narratives. At least part of the time when he was composing these works, he felt like Pegasus harnessed to a plow and, like a plowhorse, saw it as his chief duty to make as directly as possible for the end of the furrow.

To introduce Musset's prose works in this way seems an invitation to the reader to pass over the stories to reach the poems and plays all the sooner, but anyone who did this would miss a great deal that is of literary and biographical value. *La Confession d'un enfant du siècle* in particular reaches peaks of power and intensity unsurpassed even in *Lorenzaccio.* Penetrating social commentary and criticism which are rarely thought of as characteristic of Musset's writings, enchanting descriptions, ideas on love and art, an insight into human behavior which continually surprises with its sharpness of perception—all these are to be found, presented with all his charm of manner and in a style far outstripping the prose writer's modest requirements as they are laid down in *Le Poète déchu.*

II *Material and Plots*

One of the earliest narratives, *L'Anglais mangeur d'opium,* published while Musset was a seventeen-year-old student, was offered to the public as a translation of Thomas de Quincey's *Confessions of an*

English Opium-Eater (first published in 1821), but Musset was too much of a creator to plod along in the footsteps of the original, and the result is more of a variation on a theme than a translation, with much of the more serious matter left out and scenes such as the ball and the duel added for their picturesqueness, speaking loudly of the literary fashions of these early Romantic years. After an interval of five years, Musset was working (in 1833) on *Le Roman par lettres* which he carried no further than the abrupt ending of the first paragraph of letter twelve. The plot has a fairy-tale theme—a traveling musician courts a princess in her German castle—but like the other incomplete narrative, *Le Poète déchu,* this handful of pages would have been a sad loss if it had not been published posthumously. Here the reader would have been the poorer for a comic gallery of caricatured courtiers and for passages where the hero speaks Musset's own philosophy of love.

Between these two fragments was written and published the work that seems the unchallengeable masterpiece of this section of Musset's writings. Indeed, its power and sincerity lift *La Confession d'un enfant du siècle* into a category all its own, separate from the *Nouvelles* and *Contes* that were to follow. The tale is that of Musset himself and of his generation, related with a passion and yet a restraint which make this both a haunting story and at the same time one of the most important documents on the emotional life of society in this period. It is true that a passing glimpse of Musset himself in disguise appears in the majority of his works, but here in the person of Octave we see him in close-up, or rather are present while he analyses his own moral and emotional disability—that is, the debauchery and cynicism which make him destroy through distrust the very love on which he pins his hopes of a cure. George Sand is said to have been well pleased with her own portrayal as Brigitte la Rose, since Musset takes on himself all the blame for the final failure of their love affair, and while the work was in process she cooperated in making it as authentic as possible by returning the letters which Musset had written her. Differing histories of their relationship followed (George Sand, *Elle et lui,* in 1859; Paul de Musset's *Lui et elle* in the same year; Louise Colet's *Lui,* published in the following year), but perhaps there can never be one single account which represents the complete truth of any relationship, and certainly Alfred seems to be striving to describe his own role as honestly as possible.

As we shall see, the plots of the *Nouvelles* often add their own reflected facets of Musset's life. In *Les Deux Maîtresses,* published with *Emmeline* in 1837, the young Valentin, wavering between the two women who attract him equally, often reminds the reader of Musset's own nature and circumstances, and the heroine of *Emmeline* is said to be modeled on Madame Jaubert. The same family provided the plot of *Le fils du Titien,* published a year later, in which Musset transports to an Italian setting an incident in his own life when he received the mysterious gift of a purse and fell in love with the donor, Aimée d'Alton. In the fictional version the hero is Titian's second son, sharing much of Musset's personality and his ideas on art and life. The plots of the two other *Nouvelles* published in this year bring us back to France, and they too owe something to the author's own experience. *Frédéric et Bernerette* relates Musset's love affair with a young actress called Louise Lebrun, and the shattering of their happiness when another of her admirers committed suicide in the Bois de Boulogne. It seems strange that this Romantic plot par excellence, with love leading to tragedy and violence, should in fact be a transposition from real life.

Margot (1838) and *Croisilles* (1839) both take us into provincial France. The first, sparked off by Musset's meeting with a young country girl who worked as a servant in a friend's house, is partly an idyll of country life and partly the story of an unconfessed and despairing love, that of Margot for her benefactress's son. She too attempts suicide, but is fished out of the river by her childhood admirer to renew the idyll in marriage to him. Alone among the *nouvelles,* *Croisilles* seems to be a story sprung mainly from Musset's own fancy. We meet the young hero wandering back along the Seine to Le Havre after successfully transacting his business affairs, only to find his father ruined and already crossing the Atlantic to America. Almost penniless, Croisilles nevertheless wins the affection of a young heiress, and she herself surmounts the problem of gaining her father's consent to the match by enlisting an old relative of Croisilles to act as fairy godmother in this fairy story. The last pages taper off in obvious weariness with the forced labor of story writing, and if the reader feels that *Croisilles* needs a final scene, he is obliged to imagine it for himself.

If Musset himself had had a fairy godmother, there would probably have been no *Contes.* As it was, shortage of money acted rather as the fairy-tale wicked stepmother, and after *Histoire d'un merle blanc* had appeared in 1842 with comic and occasionally bitter satire of the Romantic men of letters, 1843 brought *Pierre et Camille,* the charming story of a girl born deaf and therefore in those days dumb, who eventually finds happiness in marriage with another deaf-mute and in education to help her make contact with the world of sound. *Le secret de Javotte* (1844) savors a little of Spanish plots. Honor and a slanderous tongue play on the slightest of events to draw two men into a fatal duel. Another blood bath brings to an end *Les Frères Van Buck, légende allemande,* a slight story telling of the love of a pair of inseparable brothers for the same girl. A year later, in 1845, Musset took his readers on another visit to the world of Frédéric and Bernerette, a world so like that of *La Bohème* that it does not seem out of place if memories of Puccini's music echo in one's ears as the story is read. *Mimi Pinson, profil de grisette* has a less tragic plot than the *nouvelles* based on Musset's adventure with Louise Lebrun, though here too he shows how starvation and gaiety elbow each other in the *grisette*'s world. Mimi Pinson pawns her only dress and so her means of going out to work—to help a destitute friend, but this time the tale ends happily with a wealthy baron coming to the rescue and the two girls making merry in the elegant Café Tortoni.

It was eight years before the publication of the next short story. *La Mouche* appeared in installments bridging 1853 and 1854 in time to entertain the readers of *Le Moniteur Universel* over Christmas and New Year. Here Musset takes a field that was new to him in his short-story writing, French history pinpointed at the court of Louis XV at Versailles. A knowledgeable reconstruction of the palace and its courtiers takes on a fairy-tale atmosphere as Musset charmingly and wittily relates the adventures of the Chevalier de Vauvert, who must regain the king's favor to obtain his commission and so the hand of his sweetheart. This was the last of the short stories to be known until very recently, when a short, fantastic tale was unearthed, telling of the love of a boy for a figure on an ornamental church clock.[1]

Eighteenth-century Versailles and the Venice of Titian's son are the furthest that Musset strays in his prose narratives from his own age and his own haunts. His imagination was not tempted to wander back to the Middle Ages that fascinated so many authors of his time, as they did Hugo in *Notre-Dame de Paris;* nor, after the exotic and mocking fantasies of his *Contes d'Espagne et d'Italie,* did the fashionably colorful Mediterranean settings often lure him from the softer light of French skies. From this point of view he is out of step with the main ranks of the Romantics, and another characteristic of his plots takes him even further out of line. As we have seen, suspenseful events rarely follow each other hotfoot in his work as in a Dumas novel or a Hugo play, and apart from several violent deaths, the incidents themselves are rarely gripping enough to hold a reader's attention unaided. In *Les Deux Maîtresses,* for example, we do little but wander with the hero through the streets of Paris and sit with him in salons or his own garden. Avoiding melodrama and the exotic, Musset's narratives ignore two of the chief Romantic methods of riveting the reader's attention. How, then, do they succeed in pinning him to his armchair, as many of them seem to me to do?

III *The Role of Nature*

One powerful attraction, though not the chief, lies for me in something which is perhaps not often considered an important aspect of Musset's work—that is, the settings to his stories, both where they are purely visual and where they take the form of commentary on society. As far as descriptive backgrounds are concerned, nature might have surged back into French literature with the oncoming Romantic movement, but it has been said that it meant little to Musset, one of the most Parisian writers. It is true that, compared with Lamartine or Hugo, he rarely announces his affection for nature with fanfares. Even when he speaks of nature in *La Confession d'un enfant du siècle* as his "dear mother" (p. 564), or describes how Octave's greatest pleasure was to take his mistress into the summer countryside, "the sight of nature in its splendor always having been for me the most powerful of aphrodisiacs". (p. 563), this might well be no more than artificial convention. Yet if a reader takes the time to study what these narratives reveal of Musset's appreciation of nature, he will see, I think, that this aspect of his writings has been underestimated because of the subtlety and discretion with which he uses description. Again in the *Confession* Octave tells how he used to spend hours each morning gazing from his window at the landscape of valley and village before him (p. 589), and there seems every reason to believe that this is as autobiographical as the other details of his portrayal. One of the clearest proofs that this is so lies in the number of images taken from nature that can be found when Musset is writing with great intensity, as in the second chapter of the *Confession,* which we shall examine later on in this chapter.

Inevitably Musset, with his Classical education, sometimes looks at nature through literature and legend, as when he speaks of the powerlessness of reality to withstand the dreams of a young heart and draws a parallel with oak trees from even the most gnarled of which a dryad slipped out (p. 564). At other times, contemporary fashions in scenery are reflected. It is difficult to tell whether the description of sixteen-year-old Emmeline's transports of joy when she sees the Swiss mountains is satirical or not. Satire seems out of keeping with Musset's sympathetic treatment of his heroine, but her reactions are almost too typical of the Romantic vogue for wild, craggy scenes to be true. When she saw the mountains, the story tells, her companions thought she had lost her reason, so wild was her delight. She shouted out and leaped from the carriage; she had to go and plunge her face into the springs flowing from the rocks. She wanted to climb up to the peaks, or down to the torrents in the precipices; she gathered stones and pulled up moss; one day she went into a chalet and refused to leave it; they almost had to carry her out by force and, when she was back in the carriage once more, she called out in tears to the country people: "Oh my friends, you are letting them take me away!" (p. 673). The Rhineland setting for the brothers' fight in *Les Frères Van Buck* is very much of this type, with twilight succeeding sunset in a pine wood overlooking a valley, but here there are enough observed details—the rough bark of the trees, the grasses bending under the dew—to save the description from being a hackneyed copy of so many Romantic passages. In fact, Musset's personal observation of nature rarely seems clouded by literary memories or distorted by contemporary taste.

Not surprisingly, nature and Paris often meet and fuse in his backgrounds. In the *Confession* fourteen-year-old Octave rests his elbows on his window sill to watch a scanty-leaved poplar swaying in the wind and, taking it as a representative of the whole of nature, makes a vow to keep his independence. Paris, a cloudless spring day, and the scent and blossoms of a chestnut tree in the Tuileries make up another enchanting but typically concise vignette, more compelling than any travel poster *(Bernerette,* p. 715); and section eight of *Emmeline* opens with all the essence of sunny autumn mornings in the capital compressed into a couple of lines. There are other occasions when nature subtly invades an interior scene with warm, scented air from the garden. Scents rarely seem to pass unnoticed in these brief passages.

Critics sometimes appear to forget that this Parisian sparrow was also very well acquainted with the countryside, as the short stories constantly remind their reader. Sometimes there are delightful landscapes with houses, such as Emmeline's Moulin de May with its long avenue of trees, the Walk of Sighs. Obviously Musset was as sensitive as any other Romantic to the sway of surroundings on emotions, for he relates how a lonely stroller through this seemingly endless gallery of trees feels both uneasy and delighted at the solitude, and then sinks into daydreams despite himself (p. 675). Many of the passages depicting the countryside proper are on a larger scale than nature's brief invasions into the city scene, but again one of their characteristics, in that age of

[43]

long literary purple patches, is restraint and economy. The episode that preludes Margot's attempt at suicide is set in the park of a country house in autumn. Musset provides his reader with just enough details for all the senses to be aware of the landscape—the golden leaves still hanging from the branches, the gentle softness of the wind, the birds busy with late courtship, the mellow warmth of the sun—but not a single line more than is necessary, in contrast with the purely decorative description of, for example, Chateaubriand's tone poems to autumn.

Restraint does not imply lack of power, and there is one particularly dramatic landscape in *Frédéric et Bernerette* where the moon rises and suddenly transforms the dark forest of Montmorency:

The moon was rising; it emerged slowly from the dark masses and, as it climbed higher, the clouds seemed to flee before it. Below the plateau there stretched a valley where the wind moaned dully in a sea of swaying dark foliage; the eye could distinguish nothing there, and within fifteen miles of Paris one might have been on the edge of a ravine in the Black Forest. Suddenly the orb rose above the horizon; an immense sheet of light spread over the tree-tops and filled the space in a second; the groves of full-grown trees, the clumps of chestnut trees, the clearings, the roads, the hills were all outlined in the distance as if by enchantment. (pp. 709-10)

If a set of jigsaws existed of hackneyed Romantic landscapes, forests and moonlight would occur again and again, but to me Musset's use of them spells fresh observation and the eye of a trained artist rather than stereotyped convention.

Very much the same type of scenery with rocks, forests, storms, and moonlight, echoing in prose Beethoven's *Pastoral Symphony,* provides a background to a number of key scenes in the *Confession,* heightening the human emotions which are in play. Again the descriptions are full of sounds and scents as well as sights, and yet free from Romantic wordiness. Musset uses surprisingly few adjectives; often those he chooses convey feelings or atmosphere rather than visual description. Octave and Brigitte play out one crucial scene against a background of "gloomy avenues" and "lonely rocks," for instance. One of the most memorable pieces of landscape painting is the garden scene which preludes the first lovemaking in the *Confession.* In the space of a few lines, Musset creates a tone poem, recalling Berlioz' *Nuits d'été,* of a moonlit, scented night fusing with the lovers' emotions as they rise to a climax without one word being spoken (p. 600). Nature, then, is described with power and lyrical beauty in these narratives, but it is never merely irrelevant decoration; rather, Musset introduces it at moments of crisis to fuse with the emotional situation and intensify it.

IV *Exotic Settings*

If nature plays a far more important role in the short stories than one would have expected from reading the critics, as we have already noted, Musset makes surprisingly little use of one of the most immediately attractive features displayed in the Romantic shop window—exotic local color. Spain and Italy in particular offered the Romantics all the wealth of color and passion that they craved, and the greater the success of Hugo's group, the more authors traveled, in imagination or in fact, beyond the Apennines or the Pyrenees. We shall see in the chapter dealing with poetry how Musset pokes fun at this Mediterranean mania, and we have already seen that only once does he choose a southern setting for a story. In *Le fils du Titien* the local color is applied vividly, but it is never plastered on to the background in the way that makes some works by less skilled contemporaries look like travel posters run riot. Often these same second-rank Romantic authors never rise above the superficial and the hackneyed in their portrayal of foreign lands, and here again Musset's superiority is clear. He is not content to move on to the set a mandolin, a gondolier, and a palace, which for many Romantics were sufficient to establish the place as Venice. The pages glow with descriptions of costumes and physical appearance: Pippo in his gold-embroidered shirt, scarlet-plumed hat, doublet of rich velvet with satin sleeves; Monna Bianchina with the blonde hair and dark eyes that characterize a type of Venetian woman whose resentment is a thing to be feared. Yet Musset does not stop here. Customs as well as costumes fill in the Venetian background, and we glimpse something of the administration, of the dreaded "Lords of the Night" who were part of the police system. Historical touches, too, add depth to the picture with details such as Titian's encounter with Charles V.

Above all, a panorama of the town itself is unfolded before our eyes in a passage which, as though Musset's pen were a movie camera, conveys action and movement as well as color, shape, and sound. As the frigate stationed at the harbor entrance fires the six o'clock gun, Pippo, waiting for his mysterious visitor, sees the pale blue light of dawn tinting his window. The deserted canal and silent palaces are wrapped in mist. The breeze scarcely ruffles the water; in the distance one or two sails can be seen. Only the angel of St. Mark's campanile high above the town rises from the mist, its golden wings glinting in the first rays of sunshine. Meanwhile, the countless churches are ringing the angelus, and the pigeons winging toward the corn scattered for them in the main square. The mists lift a little, the sun shines out; fishermen begin to stir, cleaning their boats and taking up, each in turn, a national song. Just then the prow of a gondola glitters in the sun, and the boat speeds over the water, bringing Pippo's mistress to his door. Musset's use of local color is not only thorough and discreet but also enticing enough to make the reader long to take the next flight to Venice.

V *French Settings*

Eighteenth-century Versailles is re-created with the same enchantment in *La Mouche* where, to the nonhistorian at least, there seems to be a fund of background information on customs and furnishings. Yet, factual as they are, the palace and the Trianon take on such an air of delicate fantasy at Musset's touch that they might well belong to a fairy tale. There is none of the heaviness here of some of the wearisomely long and detailed descriptions which some nineteenth-century authors produced in imitation of Walter Scott. Apart from a few such excursions, the short stories might well share as a subtitle "La vie quotidienne en France à l'époque d'Alfred de Musset." In the provinces we glimpse farmhouse life, sometimes idyllic as in *Margot*, sometimes wretched as in the *Confession*. More often we are allowed to enter into the daily round of a stately country house—the huntsman leaving in the mist of dawn, the walks in the park, the evenings after dinner spent with playing cards, music, or tapestry work, the candles brought at bedtime, and the sudden baying of dogs announcing a latecomer in the night.

Yet portrayals of country life are far outnumbered by sketches of Paris which together form a bustling panorama of life in the capital. Very few of these are merely descriptions of places, though there are captivating pictures of nineteenth-century interiors, especially salons with their hangings and elegant furnishings. The first pages of *Margot* alone offer a social historian a fascinating account of an upper middle-class household of Musset's day. In most of these passages, however, the figures are far more important than the landscapes, and the picture is all the more comprehensive for the ease with which Musset, himself both a student and a member of fashionable social circles, moves between the Paris of the wealthy and that of the *grisettes* who continually balanced on the edge of starvation.

VI *Social Commentary*

After following the characters of the short stories around Paris, there is little we do not know about high-society entertainment. We eavesdrop on social evenings, watching the "galop," the dance of the moment; visit the opera and the opera ball; join a riding party to the forest of Montmorency; and learn of life in the theater wings from *Le Secret de Javotte.* Valentin, courting his two mistresses, takes the reader on a tour of the lover's Paris, driving down the Avenue des Champs-Elysées in the sunset in a carriage draped with silk and drawn by two grays; reading or talking under the shady trees of a country inn near the Bois de Romainville at daybreak. Pieced together, this picture of elegant society not only forms an attractive background but is extremely interesting as Musset's view of one of the worlds in which he moved. His second world, sometimes just as gay, is at the same time more touching, and reveals a social awareness and compassion which are rarely mentioned when his work is analyzed. It is not that Musset sees the aristocratic world only in the colors of pink, blue, white, and gold of the ballrooms he pictures. He perceptively notes too the plight of society girls reared only for marriage, and thrown into it and into childbirth before they have any knowledge of life. He tells how many a well-bred girl must secretly slave away at millinery to earn a little to help her family keep up appearances.

Nor does he show only the tragic side of life in the attics of Paris. The young men in his stories indulge in the same sort of madcap pranks as Fantasio does in the play of that name and as Musset and his friends did on the Quai Malaquais. He writes too of the parties in student lodgings where *grisettes* were among the guests, of the cafés and dances they frequented, and the quieter evenings spent reading poetry and listening to songs. Mingled with these gay scenes, there are passages as unforgettable as the account of Mimi Pinson's friend Rougette, pale and weak with illness and starvation, wrapped in a shabby dressing gown, her hair undone, clinging to the wall as she tries to make her way to a mailbox to send an appeal for help. There are sharp-sighted analyses too of the background of the *grisette* and her formation. Dumas, with his play *The Lady of the Camellias,* first performed in 1852, was by no means the first to show how the faults of society can drag a woman down to a plight as pathetic as Rougette's.

In fact, Musset is constantly a social critic as well as a painter of charming scenes. He comments on the social cynicism which spoils relations between the sexes, making the conduct of an affair as automatic and as devoid of feeling as a dance routine. By drawing a contrast with Renaissance Italy, he exposes the so-called virtue of contemporary society as mere hypocrisy. The invasion of English ways may have been to blame for some change in manners, and the mania for English imports—from hotel porters to horses—provokes Musset's barbs. Though the short stories may rank behind Musset's poetry and plays in some respects, they reveal perhaps more clearly than any other part of his work a social awareness and a social conscience with which this supposed butterfly of the Romantic group is rarely credited.

VII *Character Portrayal*

If this serious aspect of some of Musset's writings has been soft-pedaled, it is generally acknowledged that he has a clearer insight into the workings of the human heart than most of his contemporaries. In his introduction to the section of narrative prose works in his edition of Musset's complete works, Van Tieghem suggests that the characters who people these stories are not very striking; it is true, I think, that few of them remain in the memory as vividly as characters from the dramatic works do. Nevertheless, not even the disliked medium of the short story could blunt Musset's skill at portraying human beings. There is a comic scattering of grotesque figures, for instance, very similar to those who walk the boards of his theater. Sometimes these are purely laughable, like the "walking barrel" of a courtier and the elderly ladies-in-waiting, "beplumed like mules," who flock round their mistress, in *Le Roman par lettres.*

Others are more developed and more sinister, like Mademoiselle Ursule in *Margot,* a sister character in some ways to Dame Pluche in *On ne badine pas avec l'amour.* Tall and angular, sanctimonious and imperious, she cheats her mistress and, like Balzac's main characters, stamps the imprint of her nature on her surroundings. "Thanks to her, there was not a speck of dust in the house; everything was clean, tidy, scrubbed, brushed, the furniture in order, the linen white, the dishes sparkling, the clocks keeping good time; all this was essential to the housekeeper so that she could scold as much as she would and queen it in all her glory" (p. 730). M. Godeau, the financier in *Croisilles,* with his rounded paunch, short legs, immense wig, and triple chin, combines social satire with fun: "At the moment he had the gout, which was as fashionable in those times as migraine is now. Lying on a chaise longue, his eyes half closed, he drowsed in a boudoir. The mirror panels which surrounded him repeated majestically on all sides his enormous person; bags full of gold covered his table; around him the furniture, the wainscoting, the doors, the locks, the chimney, the ceiling were gilded; his coat was the same; I am not sure that his brain was not gilded too." (p. 721)

Other, more sympathetic types who figure in the plays appear briefly here. *Le Secret de Javotte* has a slight sketch of one of the charming, solicitous mothers who were probably modeled on Madame de Musset; and Desgenais, the "reasonable" friend, argues with Octave in the *Confession* as Spark does with Fantasio in the play of that name. Like every other part of Musset's work, however, the stories belong to a world of youth, and almost every character of any importance is a young man or a young woman. Above all, Musset shows his subtlety and understanding in portraying the reactions of young people in love. In fact, the *nouvelles* between them take us through the intricacies of a lover's progress. In *Les Deux Maîtresses* we see the gradual process by which Valentin falls in love. In *Emmeline* we read of the almost telepathic understanding and shared feelings which sometimes prelude love, and then of the spell of awkwardness which can sometimes jangle the relationship of two people on the threshold of admitting their feelings for each other; reaching the climax of their affair, Emmeline finds what is for her the supreme joy of seeing her lover's face transfigured by mingled love, respect, adoration, doubt, and fear.

Perhaps the most moving passage in this calendar of love is the one describing, after the peak of bliss, the high plateau of happiness that comes from shared daily life. This is surprisingly unlike the alternating storms and raptures that make up ideal love in most Romantic literature.

Familiarity, so they say, leads to satiety; this is possible; but it leads to confidence, forgetfulness of oneself, and when love survives familiarity it has nothing else to fear. Lovers who see each other only after long intervals are never sure of being in sympathy with each other; they are prepared to be happy, they want to convince themselves that they are happy, and they search for something that cannot be found, that is words to express their feelings. Those who live together have no need to express anything; they share feelings at the same moment, they exchange looks, they press each other's hand as they walk along; they alone know a delightful pleasure, the sweet langor of the day after; they rest from love's transports in the ease of friendship: these charming relationships have sometimes come to my mind when I have seen two swans on a stretch of mirror-clear water letting themselves drift on the current. *(Frédéric et Bernerette*, p. 712)

Finally comes the blow of love's dying away, "the deepest wound that death deals us here below before striking us down." Musset may be a

Romantic in his high estimation of the power of love, but his picture of its everyday happiness is far more realistic than one would have expected, and all the more memorable because of that. Indeed, his shrewdness in pinpointing typical human reactions is evident throughout the stories, and often introduces a wryly comic note. Valentin talks of "some of those phrases prepared beforehand that one learns by heart and never uses," and later he "did as all men do; not being able to renounce his folly, he tried to make it seem reasonable." All the concision and pithiness of the eighteenth-century epigram has clearly been handed down to Musset.

If we look first at the portrait gallery of heroines, we see what truth there is in the critical cliché that Musset must be considered with Racine and Marivaux for his uncanny knowledge of the way in which a woman's mind works. His Margot and Mimi come to life before the reader's eyes in spite of the fact—a fact that is astonishing in this Romantic period with its long pen-pictures—that we are told hardly anything of their personal appearance. When we are given an inkling of how they look, the glimpse sometimes brings George Sand to mind. The two mistresses sharing Valentin's affections both have large, dark eyes, and so too does Mimi Pinson who, with her black dress, prides herself on her Spanish look. The darker the eyes the better, in a *grisette,* writes Musset. His heroines are scarcely ever presented in lyrical descriptions, but instead there is a penetrating realism that notices, for instance, the young widowed seamstress's look of habitual weariness. The analysis of this same character shows a subtle understanding of niceties of situation which does indeed rival Marivaux. Madame Delaunay cannot afford to allow herself a flirtation, Musset points out. Ladies of leisure can defend themselves in such skirmishes and can turn to other distractions when necessary. "But Madame Delaunay was too busy, too sedentary, saw too little company, worked too much at sewing which allows time for dreaming and sometimes gives rise to it; she was too poor, in a word, to allow anyone to kiss her hand" *(Les Deux Maîtresses,* p. 659).

Madame Delaunay and all the other heroines, except Brigitte in the *Confession* and perhaps the two *grisettes* Bernerette and Mimi, are more shadowy figures than those who people the *Comédies et Proverbes,* but it is only by such a comparison that they seem to lack force. Certainly they are always convincing: Emmeline the tomboy with her love of solitude, resembling George Sand as a girl; the Marquise de Parnes, swayed chiefly by the instinctive pride which prevailed over her passions; and the slightly unpleasant figure of Madame de Vernage in *Le Secret de Javotte,* giving Musset the chance to denounce the power for evil of a slanderous coquette who kept up only the outward show of religion. The pride, vanity, and false religion which could destroy a woman's sincerity in her dealings with others and bring tragedy are dealt with fully in *On ne badine pas avec l'amour,* but throughout the works there are traces of Musset's concern with this feminine flaw.

Like Racine and Marivaux, then, Musset has an almost uncanny ability to depict women's minds and emotions, but, unlike their works, his are not dominated by the heroines. Usually his stories and plays gain from having their main protagonists, both male and female, of equal stature and vigor. Yet for the reader who wishes to discover the author in his writings, the heroes have a special interest. Musset was perfectly capable of creating characters who shared no part of his own nature, as his works amply prove, but Frédéric and Octave, Valentin and Pippo have an added richness because they reflect facets of Musset's own personality, especially the central problem of his life to which he never found a satisfactory solution. Apart from the full-length portrait of the *Confession,* almost all these self-reflections are found in the *nouvelles,* emphasizing how much more than the *contes* these meant to Musset. It is true that the *contes* show a fleeting likeness of him in the heroine's worldwearied father in *Pierre et Camille* and in Armand de Berville with his precocious experience of the world in *Le Secret de Javotte,* but in general the author seems to stand further outside these stories than in any other part of his work.

Until the fragments of *Le Poète déchu* were published, readers were deprived of a fascinating account of Musset's debut in the literary world as he saw it himself. Here we see him elated with apparently all the world at his feet, dabbling in debauchery but with no real knowledge of life, only to be plunged into what was for him both a great sorrow and an invaluable experience, educating his understanding of literature and art as well as of life. It is difficult to think of another author of this period who could write of his own experience with such frankness, modesty and, above all, lack of exaggeration. "I have not told you the details of my romance. Yet the story, if I wrote it, would be as good as any other such; but what is the use? My mistress was dark-haired; she had huge eyes; I loved her, she left me; I grieved and wept for four months; is there any need to say more?" (p. 648).

The introductory pages to *Les Deux Maîtresses* are well worth studying for their analysis of the hero's character, especially the dual nature which split Valentin into two different people, leading a double existence and finding in his two mistresses "the contrast which delighted him." Like Musset, then, Valentin is "a constant contradiction," and in other ways too there are similarities. As a child, Valentin is a dreamer with a passion for everything brilliant and golden, from sunlight to gold itself; at school he feels an intense need to distinguish himself; and as a young man his tastes belong to a financial situation much superior to his own as a "lawyer without a brief, a common profession nowadays." The greatest force for good in him is his affection for the mother who spoils him. Perhaps the most attractive features of this profligate dreamer are his good nature and the candor which makes him detest the vanity and hypocritical show of "virtue" which Madame de Parnes displays. An open avowal of love brings a show of anger from her, but she is pleased enough to listen to what she takes for compliments in disguise, preening herself meanwhile in the mirror.

Every characteristic which Valentin reveals is a reflection of his creator and, in *Emmeline,* Gilbert follows the same pattern with his mixture of shyness and the extreme frankness of manners and speech which offends Emmeline's sister. It is "le Fils du Titien," though, who does the most to complement the portrait of Musset as we have seen it in *Les Deux Maîtresses.* He has the same frankness and combines strangely contrasting strength and weakness of character. Nonchalant over everyday affairs, he is unshakable on matters which are important to him. Like Musset, he leads a life of debauchery which is burning him out as surely as the symbolical fire in the opening scene of the story razed the Venetian palace and, again like Musset, it was boredom rather than natural viciousness which propelled him toward this life.

All these traits are gathered together in *La Confession d'un enfant du siècle,* where Musset looks at his own nature in a full-length mirror and allows us to study the reflection with him, although we must remember that the image is distorted by his determination to shoulder all the blame for the breakdown of his affair with George Sand. We see again the attractive straightforwardness which, Octave says, makes it impossible for him to tell any woman whom he despises that he has any feeling for her, even when both know that this is merely a convention. Most of his study, however, consists of a terrifying analysis of how boredom, cynicism, and debauchery can destroy a personality. This is not the preaching of someone who has never known the ravages he describes, but a case history written by a man still suffering from them. Musset may not have been a success as a medical student, but here he is admirable in his direct, clinical approach to his own emotional and moral illness.

The outlines of the story have been traced in the biographical chapter, but every page of the *Confession* is worth reading and rereading for the fresh understanding it brings of the personal problems which are seldom far from the surface of any of Musset's works. We read of the influence of libertine books and of growing religious doubts; the "mal du siècle" incarnate in a prostitute; the disillusion which finds that even the supposed glamor of the dissolute life turns out to be merely sordidness. In an important passage which brings *Lorenzaccio* to mind, Octave relates how he forced the mask of a blasé cynic over his own features. "There were almost constantly present within me one man laughing and another weeping. There was a constant contradiction between my head and my heart." Later, when the mask has almost become the man, he diagnoses the death of willpower brought on by debauchery and draws horrific pictures of the man who is destroyed by vice. If greatness in a Greek tragedy was measured partly by the ability to arouse pity and terror, then in parts of the *Confession* Musset seems to me on a par with the great tragedians who showed with compassion the depths to which a human being can fall.

A glint of brightness is introduced by Octave's hope that human love may be strong enough to restore him to health, another theme that recurs throughout Musset's work. Like George and Alfred, Brigitte and Octave had been too badly scarred by earlier experience for this hope to become reality, and Octave, bewildered by his own cruelty, sees himself torturing his mistress with his taunts and his frenzies. If this novel were centered on the problem of the malaise of the early nineteenth century alone, it could have only a limited interest. Its stature comes from Musset's ability to penetrate to situations which are universal. Writers from St. Paul to those of the twentieth century have touched on similar ground to Musset when he questions himself in Octave. "To do evil! this then was the role that Providence had imposed on me! To do evil! I whose conscience told me, even in the thick of my ragings, that I was good! ... I who ... had I committed a crime and spilt blood with these very hands, would still have reiterated that my heart was not guilty, that it was a mistake, that it was not I myself who was acting thus, but my fate, my evil genius, some being or other who lived within me but was not born there" (p. 634).

VIII *Themes*

This tormented, inward-looking aspect of Musset is probably the one most commonly known, but the short stories prove that he is more than just the heart or the nervous system of the Romantic period. Alfred de Vigny is generally recognized as the man of thought among the French Romantics, but we have already seen that Musset could cast a sharply critical eye on society, and the stories disclose other ideas in plenty, although their development is never allowed to slow down the narrative. *Le Fils du Titien,* for instance, touches not only on the history of art but also on its philosophy, especially the artist's difficult task of striking a balance between his creative work and his enjoyment of life. Musset seems to approve Raphael's decision to throw the former overboard for the other. He certainly believes that a piece of work, artistic or literary, carried out in a rush is likely to be no worse than one which has been painstakingly touched up. Many students might find comfort in the account of how the hero's thesis in *Frédéric et Bernerette* "was finished in a hurry and was none the worse for that" (p. 705). Whether one agrees with this theory or not, there is valuable literary criticism in plenty in the narrative prose works, and Musset chooses the most difficult type of literature to assess, that which was contemporary. Anyone interested in the battle of the Romantics with the rearguard Classics, the typical Romantic man of letters, or a caricatural pen sketch of Victor Hugo and George Sand, has only to turn to *Le Poète déchu* and *Histoire d'un merle blanc.*

In these passages and in the *Lettres de Dupuis et Cotonet,* Musset shows himself a witty and perspicacious critic, but in his stories as in his poems and plays he emerges above all as the philosopher, almost the priest, of love. The language of religion is used again and again in speaking of love, as in the passionate lyrical apostrophe which opens Chapter XI of the *Confession.* Yet this is not a heretical religion setting itself up for the worship of a false god but, for Musset, an integral part of the true God and of his universe. Love is a divine tear dropped to the earth as man's only consolation; it is a fallen angel unable to leave the beauty it has created. In Letter VIII of *Le Roman par lettres* Prévan explains to Louise, long before the popular song writers caught hold of the idea, that it is in fact love which is the moving force of the whole world. Such passages sound trite when they are analyzed, but in the French text they have a rare beauty which halts the reader in his tracks and which seems too fragile to survive translation. The very kernel of *Le Roman par lettres,* beneath the flimsy plot, consists of a treatise on love. We read, again expressed in exquisite prose, of the difference between platonic and sensual love and of the tragic impossibility of any real contact between two human beings, even those who love each other—a favorite theme of twentieth-century authors. Even so, Musset says, a man is happy if he has a momentary encounter with the woman he has seen in his dreams at some cross-road of the dark waste land of life.

[54]

It is difficult to talk of this central theme in Musset's work without making him seem a sentimentalist, which to my mind he is not. Love is not mainly for him a "romantic" affair of moonlight and roses, lyrically though he can write. Nothing could be more idealistic and yet realistic at the same time than the description in Chapter V of the *Confession* of the mental, spiritual, and physical union of two beings who love each other. This is poetic prose, but the subject matter is as close to real life as a marriage guidance council leaflet.

IX *Narrative Technique*

Unique among Musset's works for the space it gives to ideas, the *Confession* also stands apart from the short stories in the way in which it is constructed. Clarity is not a quality for which the Romantic group as a whole is usually praised, but the different stages of this semiautobiography are marshaled in an orderly way and divided into sections so that the reader is left with a satisfying impression of clear construction. The story is well rounded off too, as Octave's post-chaise carries him away from Paris and he casts a last look at the city where he has left Brigitte to happiness with her new lover. The *Confession* meant a great deal to Musset, and no doubt this explains the care he took over its construction, as his dislike of having to waste his time and gifts on short-story writing explains the brusqueness with which many of the *contes* and *nouvelles* are brought to a stop, as though the author were weary of pulling his puppets' strings and could not bear to spend another minute with them. *Croisilles,* the last *nouvelle* to be written, has the most telescoped ending of all. As was mentioned earlier in this chapter, when Paul de Musset struggled to persuade his brother to add the final scene which would have taken scarcely two hours to write, Alfred refused point blank to add a single word to the manuscript, and his only reply when people reproached him later with the abrupt ending was to rub his hands and say "Finis prosae."

Emmeline ends a little less brusquely, but the story might be criticized for the sudden introduction in the closing chapter of a totally new character, who is used to bring the plot to an end. Yet the incident that served to provide this story was after all transposed from real life, and real life has a habit of being less symmetrical than fiction. What is more surprising is the supernatural element at the close of *Les Frères Van Buck,* where the two brothers in their death agony see a spectral form moving toward them in the twilight and, recognizing their mother, clasp each other in a last embrace. Nothing could be more typical of short stories written at this period, but Musset rarely had any truck with such ghostly melodrama, even in the Germanic setting which invited it at this time. Sometimes, then, these works end with a jarring abruptness which makes the reader feel that there may be some truth in the generally held impression that Musset's method of work was like Pippo's in *Le Fils du Titien:* "Without thinking and without pausing, he wrote a sonnet in great haste." Musset himself fosters this idea of haphazardness in *Emmeline* when he greets the climax, the heroine's fortnight of happiness, with: "A fortnight is a very short time, is it not? I began this story without thinking about that, and I see that, now I have reached the moment which inspired me to take up my pen, I have nothing to say about it, except that it was very short."

Nothing apart from the occasional ending mars the polish of Musset's narrative technique, however. Every page has the simplicity and clarity that are the heritage of La Fontaine's countrymen and in addition a charm, ease, and wit which are Musset's own. His plays are, for the most part, an "armchair theater" and his short stories might well have as a subtitle "Armchair tales" because of the air of intimacy that is created between author and reader. Musset frequently addresses the imaginary occupant of the armchair opposite his own (significantly, as "Madame" rather than "Monsieur"), teasing her and claiming the narrator's privilege of professing not to know all the details of his story—"You will understand, Madame, that I was not in the summerhouse, and from the moment the blinds were drawn it was impossible for me to see any more." There are comic and satirical touches in plenty, though not in such profusion as in the plays, and charming tableaux such as that of Margot, overawed by the splendors of Madame Doradour's Louis XV bathroom, and gazing at the cherubs, the griffons, and the Boucher nymphs.

X *Style*

The style in these short stories as a whole is an effective mingling of a descriptive ability which can capture Spring and youth in one short phrase such as that which talks of the hero "setting out one morning on one of those beautiful days when everything young goes out-of-doors without knowing why," and a reticence extremely unusual in the Romantic period. At a time when almost every page had a lyrical effusion or a descriptive rhapsody, Musset refuses to be drawn into unnecessary detail. What good is it relating how Frédéric and Bernerette spent their time, he asks, since one sentence suffices? "They were in love, they lived together; this state of affairs lasted about three months." Indeed, he sees it as sacrilege to attempt word-pictures of lovers' feelings. "What comes from the heart can be put down in writing, but not the heart itself" (*Emmeline*).

Yet if Musset had decided ideas on the limits of what could be expressed, he could and did use alliteration to capture the sounds of nature, as in his description of the wind blowing on a gloomy night, in the second paragraph of Chapter V in the *Confession.* What is more unusual is the way in which he imitates in *Le Secret de Javotte* the voice of a *grisette*-turned-actress and mistress of a rich benefactor. At one moment she is talking naturally and volubly, using expressions that still have an aroma of the cabbages she had lived on in her poverty. In the next, she remembers to drawl out the phrases of conventional society in a voice like that of a duchess with a bad cold.

In the short stories, then, which on the whole represented hard and disagreeable toil to Musset, he uses his style as a tool, economically and unobtrusively though with a skill which shows the master craftsman. The characteristics which we have noted—ease, charm, simplicity, and discretion—sometimes make one think more of the habitué of an eighteenth-century salon than the onetime spoiled darling of the Romantic group. Again it is the *Confession* which forms a towering exception to the rest of the narrative prose works. In the great second chapter none of the qualities already mentioned are lost, but in addition there is a rhetorical power and a passion which rival those of Victor Hugo. This is not the calm prose more commonly found in prerevolutionary France, it is the inflamed language that caught fire from the blaze of the political and then the literary revolution. In this chapter Musset pulls out all the stops that are available to him, both of rhythm and color; those provided by Classical mythology and rhetoric, and those liberated by Romanticism. Above all it is a vividly pictorial style, scenes and portraits following each other in steady succession as on the walls of an art gallery. After the defeat of the French at Waterloo, for instance,

there sat at the summit of a ruined world a young generation full of anxiety. All these children were drops of a feverish blood which had saturated the earth; they were born at the heart of war, were meant for war. They had dreamed for fifteen years of the snows of Moscow and the sunlight of the pyramids. They had never left their towns, but people had told them that through each town gateway lay the road to one of the capitals of Europe. In their head they had a whole world; they looked at the earth, the sky, the street, the highways; everywhere was empty, and their parish bells were the only sound to ring out in the distance.

Such a paragraph leaves a more lasting impression than many a historian's chapter, for the general reader.

Welded into a unity which yet has great variety of pace and mood, there are Classical references such as the tax paid to Caesar, and examples of irony and anticlimax—"This was the escort [three hundred thousand young men] he needed to cross the world, and sink to his rest in a small valley on a deserted island, beneath a weeping willow." Rhetorical repetitions and heroic rhetorical questions thunder out in contrast to the usual delicate subtlety of Musset's style, relieved with interludes of imagined dialogue and the wry humor of satire.

The king of France was on his throne, peering here and there to make sure there was no bee [the emblem of Napoleon] in his tapestry hangings. Some men held out their hat to him, and he gave them money; others showed him a crucifix, and he kissed it; others merely shouted great sonorous names in his ears, and he told those to go into his great hall because the echoes rang out well there; others again showed him their old cloaks from which they had carefully removed the bee motif, and to these he gave a new suit.

There is personification. "Death herself was so beautiful then, so great, so magnificent in her smoking crimson! She looked so like hope, she cut down such green ears of corn that it was as though she had become young herself in the process, and no one believed in old age any longer." This chapter was after all no mere literary exercise for Musset, but a question of the spiritual life and death of himself and his generation and, as in one of the key scenes of *Lorenzaccio* which explains how the hero's personality was destroyed, a whole series of extended images springs up from Musset's usually restrained prose. In a simile France is compared to a weary traveler, and there are metaphors such as: "At the sound of his [Napoleon's] fall, the half-dead powers rose up from their sick beds, and, stretching out their hooked legs, all the royal spiders tore Europe into shreds, and made themselves Harlequin coats from Caesar's purple mantle." This recurring disillusion and bitterness recalls the outcries of twentieth-century postwar generations—the "angry young men" of the 1950's, for instance, in Britain. Perhaps the saddest note in the chapter is struck by the two apostrophes, one to Goethe and Byron, the literary demi-gods who had handed down not hope but despair, and the second to the future generations in France, whom Musset saw peacefully reaping in cornfields bright with daisies and poppies. It is as well that foresight did not allow him to see these fields blackened and blasted by the gunfire of those later wars which plunged France into even greater distress, perhaps, than that of his own days.

XI *In Conclusion*

The *Confession* stands apart from the other narrative prose works, then, because the subject matter, both political and more strictly personal, was of the utmost importance to Musset. As a result, the structure of the work is carefully chiseled into symmetry, and the style catches fire from the intensity of his feelings to reach heights not often surpassed anywhere else in his writings. Compared with this semiautobiography, the *nouvelles* and *contes* meant to him, as we have said earlier, dreary but essential hackwork.

The reader's lot is far from dreary, however. He finds all the pleasures awaiting him that he would expect from any work by Musset—a style that has clarity, delicacy, and humor, with touches of poetry, a graceful manner, and a psychological perception which captures true reflections of human nature. As usual, too, there is the added interest of seeing Musset himself in most of the heroes and many of the plots, especially in the *nouvelles*. It would be strange if an author's dislike for the form of literature he was forced to use did not mar his work in some way, and certainly some of the stories end with an abruptness which suggests that he could hardly wait to put the final full stop. Yet in other ways Musset's craftsmanship was too sure to let him down. His plots move easily on, adorned but never hampered by reflections and descriptions. It is the descriptions themselves, descriptions of scenes and especially of society, that are the greatest surprise to anyone familiar with the conventional picture of Musset as a wit and a poet, but not knowing how close his sharply critical eye could bring his work to the social studies of Balzac and Dumas *fils*. He is not interested only in individuals and their emotions, but has a deep concern and compassion for the problems of society as a whole, without writing any solemn prefaces to draw attention to his involvement. Musset may rail bitterly against having to use narrative prose, "that rudimentary instrument with no strings, which any Tom, Dick, or Harry can strum," but if he had not done so the unforgettable *Confession* would have been lost to literature, and the reader might not have glimpsed the concern for society which appears even more clearly here than in the plays or poems.

CHAPTER 3

Poet of the "White Goddess"

I Musset and the Creative Process

I F nothing had survived of Musset's literary output except his short
stories, it is difficult to imagine that much would be known of him
today, except perhaps for a few excerpts in prose anthologies and a
reputation for the French storyteller's traditional virtues. With his
poetry, however, he steps up to take his place among the company of
the truly great. Few poets illustrate better than he does the distinction
Robert Graves makes in his *Oxford Addresses on Poetry* (London:
Cassell, 1961, p. 57) between "verse rhetoric, the product of cold
reason, and true poetry, the result of an emotional trance. For some
three thousand years, the inspiration that accompanies poetic trances
has been ascribed to a character called the Muse; and . . . what other
word can replace it?"

Whether the force that takes possession of a poet is known as the
Muse or merely as inspiration, Musset was more keenly aware of its
existence than all but a few poets in an age which made much of the
need for an artist to listen to the dictates of his own heart. Indeed,
whatever sparked off his poetic trances seems to have been for him not
"it" but "she," an almost intangible feminine presence, the "White
Goddess" as Graves calls her elsewhere. This is how Musset greets her in
La Nuit de mai: "Oh my flower! Oh my everlasting one! The only
chaste and faithful being in whom love for me still lives on! Yes, you
are here, it is you, my golden-haired one, it is you, my mistress and my
sister! And, in the depths of the night, I can feel the rays from your
golden robe that enfolds me stealing into my heart."[1] To court her
presence he would make his room a bower of candles and flowers, Paul
de Musset tells us. On the night when *La Nuit d'août* was written, the
windows stood wide open. "The candlelight played upon the flowers
which filled four great vases placed symmetrically. The muse arrived
like a young bride."

If the results had been mediocre, such preparations would rightly have been labeled a nonsensical Romantic pantomime, but the poetry that came from such evenings is well able to stand up to any test, whether it be A. E. Housman's "Does it make the hairs of one's chin bristle if one repeats it silently while shaving?" to Robert Graves's more universal distinction: "True poetic trances excite memorable images, strong personal rhythms, and a peculiar syntax which, together, transcend in emotional force the most considered rhetoric; false trances imitate these elements, but deceive no reader of sensibility."[2] Musset gives in the dedication to *La Coupe et les lèvres* a description of his experience of being gripped by creative inspiration, as well as the feeling of anticlimax into which he plummeted afterwards. "When one is working, every nerve, every fiber quivers like a lute that has just been tuned. No word is written without all one's being vibrating. (Let it be said without vanity, that is what one feels.) One is not working, one is listening, waiting. It is as though a stranger spoke to you in a low voice. ... And then, and then, it is over! Your head aches. What a strange awakening! How flat-footed you feel! How clearly you see that Vulcan has fallen from the skies."[3]

If Musset addresses his muse as the only being who is completely faithful to him, it is equally true that he on his side never seems to have wavered from his poetic integrity, a trait which should be noted in this allegedly weak and frivolous character. He had nothing but scorn for those who pour out reams of uninspired verse, and he refused to write except when poetic necessity impelled him, in spite of the fact that his friends and publishers accused him of laziness. People think that he is resting on his laurels, he writes half bitterly to Madame Jaubert in the dedication to *Silvia*. On the contrary, he has only been drowsing, nodding over an almost withered sprig of verbena, for he has no pretensions to being awarded laurel wreaths; and in this apparently lost time, silence has been revealing to him truths that it alone can teach.

II *His Ideas on the Nature of Poetry*

For Musset, then, poetry belongs to a different element from prose. To him, one seems earthbound and the other a creature of the heavens. When he is concerned with poetry, there is no trace in him of the weary and disgruntled pen-pusher who refused to spend one more instant on completing *Croisilles*. His attitude to poetry is rather that of a lover, almost a worshiper. Poetry, that immortal language, is what he loves above all, he writes in the second canto of *Namouna*. Perhaps even to admit his consuming love is blasphemy, something to be confessed only in a whisper. The reasons he gives here for his passion are not likely to be well received in post-Orwellian times, when all animals are considered equal to each other, but they are typical enough of the bourgeois-baiting Romantics who tended to see themselves as exalted beings, apart from the mob. Poetry is a God-given language, continues Musset, which has the advantage that it has never been understood by the stupid. It is beautiful and crystal clear, but is not spoken by the majority of men.

As for the substance of poetry, no one could speak more typically for his time than Musset does in this same poem. When the poet's hand writes, it does no more than transcribe what his heart has to say. Poetry is the heart melting, or reacting like a gay traveler who reaches the mountain top, stretches himself, bares his head, and draws in deep breaths. This idea is common enough, if the image is unusual, but in the following stanza (stanza v) Musset voices a much fresher thought. What does the literary value of a poem matter compared with the sheer pleasure its creation brings to the poet? The muse is beautiful even in the eyes of the crazy or ungifted artist, and her beauty lies in the love which he feels for her. The sheer pleasure that can be gained either from response to literature or from its making is an unfashionable, almost frivolous-seeming topic in the mid-twentieth century, often obscured by the weight and seriousness of criticism nurtured by psychology, but Musset is clear-sighted and unpretentious enough to bring his reader back with a jolt to one of the basic reasons for the existence of art. It is typical of Musset's lack of theorizing pomposity and of the opinions which we have just seen that his poem subtitled "In reply to this question: what is poetry?" should bear the title of "Impromptu," and that it should consist of a mere dozen lines conveying the magical fascination the poet finds in his craft rather than of an abstract discussion of poetry itself. Perhaps he comes closest to summing up his poetics in the vigorous, pithy stanzas of *Après une lecture*. What use is academic, usually posthumous admiration to a poet? he demands. One is none the less dead for being embalmed. Arousing admiration is fruitless; the only thing that matters is to be read and to give enjoyment: "Hurrah for the old-fashioned novel, hurrah for the fortunate page turned by a beauty in love, as she lies on the moss! Hurrah for the book torn by a dainty finger, splashed by the gilded bath-tap! And, let all the pedants smite their empty heads, hurrah for the melodrama that made Margot cry."[4]

Is accurate rhyming of no importance at all, then? he hears his opponents objecting; and why should a man send his son to school for fifteen years if his only judges after all that are those who wear petticoats? It is true that women are ignorant, deceitful, and vain, replies Musset, but they have beauty on their side and beauty is supreme on earth, as Plato himself declared. Light itself was made to reveal beauty to us. Boileau may have argued in his ninth "Epître" that nothing is beautiful except truth; for Musset nothing is true except the beautiful. When the first ray of sunlight lit on the world, beauty appeared; love was born of beauty and from love came harmony; it was this ray that sparked off genius, and Margot, Musset's Everywoman, is well able to recognize it instinctively, he believes. The portals of the French Academy may have trembled at this pronouncement, as indeed may those of most academic institutions even in the twentieth century. Yet Musset is not alone in thinking that true literary worth is something that is detected by the senses rather than by intellectual judgment. In *Any Honest Housewife* Robert Graves maintains that pseudo-poets can be detected instinctively, just as the average housewife can instantly distinguish between sound and rotten apples, or between a good maid and a slut.

As far as the close association of poetic truth with beauty and pleasure goes, another twentieth-century poet and critic, C. Day Lewis, holds views perhaps not very different from Musset's. In *The Poetic Image* (The Clark Lectures, Cambridge 1946. London: Cape, 1947, pp. 26-27) he affirms that "Poetic truth . . . must be accepted as the corollary and crown of poetic pleasure. It is not, like scientific truth, verifiable. . . . We judge poetic truth because it is 'operative,' because it operates upon us to cause the kind of pleasure which, in the Kantian sense, is a furtherance of life." Certainly Musset's definition of a poet insists that he can only be someone able to "déraisonner," to plunge himself into all the fantasy, joy, and grief that human experience offers. Desk-bound scribblers may win themselves reputations, but they will only be esteemed men, never poets, and their trade is the most degrading that the human brain knows. Just as Musset's "laziness" was in his own eyes something that worked for rather than against his literary creativeness, so it seems that the enjoyment of life's pleasures with which he was often reproached was for him an essential qualification for a poet.

Liberty to participate in life to the full must be matched by liberty to shape lines of poetry regardless of grammarians' dictates. "I have written bad lines, it is true," admits Musset in stanza xvii of the same poem, "but, thank Heavens! when I created them they were as I intended, and at least neither de Wailly nor Boiste [compilers of dictionaries of the French language] had a hand in them."[5] This typically Romantic idea of the poet's need for liberty occurs often in Musset's poetry, and so too does the theme of the importance of the emotional impact a piece of writing makes, this factor overriding all questions of technique. It is with this weapon, for instance, that he defends a friend in *Aux critiques du "Chatterton" d'Alfred de Vigny (Poésies posthumes)*. Of all the recurring themes that make up Musset's poetics, however, by far the best known is his insistence on the benefits that can be reaped from suffering and from remembered sorrow. Almost all selections from his verse include *La Nuit de mai,* and, if a schoolchild were unlucky, he might until recently have had the poem mangled for him by hearing it droned in class recitation. The university student under pressure is likely to pigeonhole the last two stanzas mentally in a compartment marked "quotations for examination purposes" and hurry on without really savoring the passage for itself.

Fortunately, the dialogue between the poet and his muse has a power, as well as an enchantment, which can survive this usage. The subject of grief and despair, "this sacred wound with which the black seraphim pierced the very depth of your heart," may seem an almost laughable Romantic commonplace to unsympathetically disposed twentieth-century readers, who are hardly likely to approve of the Muse's advice to let the wound expand and deepen. Yet, even for those who cannot accept the view that "The most despairing songs are the most beautiful,/And I know immortal ones which are the quintessence of a sob,"[6] there is a striking economy of language and detail, and a brutal force which is almost modern in the picture of the pelican feeding his starving children on his heart's blood, as the great poet nourishes his poems with his grief.

It is only rarely that Musset spends any poetic time discussing his own work as opposed to the general principles of poetry. His rhymes will be thought weak, he comments in the dedication to *La Coupe et les lèvres,* but he has abandoned rhyming systems, preferring to go his own sweet way. As for his contemporaries with their scheme of "rich rhymes" which demanded that rhyming syllables should contain three identical elements, "bravo! there goes another nail to imprison thought." Again it is content, not form, which matters to him. Not all his apparent apologies are disguised defenses of his own policies, however. Musset was as aware of occasional carelessness in his verse as any of his critics, although, again in *La Coupe et les lèvres,* he declares that it is pointless to revise poetry in the way an ox chews the cud. Nevertheless, in *Les Secrètes Pensées de Raphael, gentilhomme français,* he confesses his faults, not to the pedantic critics he loathed but to France itself, whose "heavenly, harmonious language [is] the language of love, so sweet that / women there wear a perpetual smile from speaking it."[7]

There is a quick reply in *Namouna* to those readers who ask if it is not the author himself who poses as the hero of his works. They are told that the characters are composite creations, the nose copied from one model, the heel from another, and so on. The accusation which Musset repudiates more fiercely than any other is that of imitating other writers. More than once he insists on his originality, however circumscribed it may be. "My glass is small, but it is from that alone that I drink" *(La Coupe et les lèvres).*[8]

This line, together with the passage about the relationship between art and suffering in *La Nuit de mai,* is probably the best known of Musset's comments on poetry, but we have seen that this is far from forming the sum total of his theories about the poet and his work. It is true that it is not a complete poetic that can be gleaned from his writings, but clearly he has decided and independent views, expressed with vigor and wit, on the essential issues of the nature and value of poetry and on what constitutes a poet. *La Nuit de mai* in particular gives the impression of a full-blown Romantic in thought as in expression, and Musset's stress on inspiration as the source and shaper of verses tallies with this. Yet on other points he repudiates Romantic doctrine. Perhaps one of the greatest surprises, in a period when writers often compared themselves to a priesthood, is his down-to-earth attitude and the humility which sees a greater tribute in having one's works torn and splashed in the bath by an avid reader than in having one's features preserved in marble busts. Above all Musset emerges as a practical poet, abhorring the shackles of academic fustiness and completely dedicated to what he considers true poetry. He is both the piper who will never play except when he calls his own tune and the court jester who judges his tales by the reaction of his hearers.

III *The Content of Ideas in Musset's Poetry*

Another shock is in store for the reader who has always thought of Musset as the poet of moonlight and roses, the poet of emotion as compared to Vigny, so often labeled as the poet of ideas among the Romantics. It would be folly to suggest that Musset should replace Vigny as the poet who gave the greatest place to thought in his lines at this period. At the same time, this aspect of the *Poésies nouvelles* in particular seems to have been unduly soft-pedaled by critics. Not only has Musset firm views on poetry, but when one looks generally at the themes which he treats it is to find him constantly returning to political and social questions, especially the situation of France in his own day. This discovery may well come as a surprise, for the most common image of Musset pictures him as one of the Romantics whose poetry was inward-looking, escaping from reality via introspection or the imagination. A closer study makes it quite clear that, while he may not write poems to greet the technological triumphs of the day, such as the arrival of the first railway, he is well aware of political events both abroad and in France, and has passionate feelings about them which raise them from journalistic material to fit perfectly into the sphere of poetic themes. *La Coupe et les lèvres,* for instance, contains in Frank's long monologue in front of the tomb a violent diatribe against the follies of the nineteenth century.

Needless to say, the concept of Musset as the poet par excellence of the Romantic love-idyll, with Lamartine, would not have arisen without cause and, although it is far from being exclusively the theme of his verse, love is often the topic which inspires him. As one studies the lines which touch on the theme, a fascinatingly clear picture emerges of the way in which Musset's ideas develop from the time when, a dazzling fledgling in Parisian society, he began his *Premières Poésies,* to the later years of the *Poésies nouvelles* with their far greater maturity. Not only do the reflective passages increase in number—this is true too of the politically inspired stanzas—but their treatment gains more and more in depth of perception, although Musset can always summon his light touch.

Even the *Premières Poésies* spring surprises on one's preconceived ideas of what to expect from a poet speaking of love in this period. Only an occasional stanza, such as stanza xlix in *Mardoche,* describes romance with all its traditional glamor and mystery—woods and lakes, balconies, masks and cloaks, moonlit nights. At the other end of the scale, *Don Paez* has lines which bring to life the delirium of love-making with a truth, allied to descriptive skill, which is eloquent of the experiences of a young rake of high society. Far outweighing these Romantic stereotypes are the passages indicating in which direction Musset's philosophy of love would develop and the high seriousness in which he would hold it. Already in *Don Paez* love is described as being flimsily attached to pleasure but securely anchored to pain (in the closing stanza of Part II), and in *Les Marrons du feu* he spends some time exploring the different role passion plays in the lives of men and women. His analysis may not be new, but it points the way to his later deep explorations of the minds of men and women. *Mardoche* too has interpolations which are half-serious comments on society and marriage, on the nineteen-year-old girl who is given a husband for a plaything just as she had dolls as playthings when she was six (stanzas xvi to xviii); and on disastrously incongruous unions he has seen contracted (lii).

Toward the end of the *Premières Poésies,* this concern for the fate of individuals in society has deepened, and the second act of *A quoi rêvent les jeunes filles* opens with an unforgettable piece of dialogue in which Laertes first points out wittily and with un-Romantic common sense the difference between the requirements of courtship and marriage, and then speaks with tenderness and concern of the bride's initiation into marriage. Above all the *Premières Poésies* contain a trumpet blast which proclaims the supremacy of love:

You will ask me if there is anything I love. I am going to reply more or less in Hamlet's fashion: Doubt what you will, Ophelia; doubt the radiance of the skies and the rose's scent; doubt virtue, day, and night; doubt everything in the world, but never love. . . .

Doubt, if you wish, the being who loves you, a woman or a dog, but not love itself. Love is everything—love and life in the sun. The great thing is to love, what does the mistress matter? What does the flagon matter, if it brings intoxication? *(La Coupe et les lèvres, Dédicace).* [9]

The thought of attempting to do justice to Musset's thoughts on love in the *Poésies nouvelles* and in some of his posthumous poems is enough to fill a commentator with despair. The themes themselves are clear enough—the blasphemy of "love-making" when no real affection exists, and the conviction that it is love which is at the very center of the universe *(Rolla);* the lover's cherished wounds; and the link, stronger than rock, diamonds, or death itself, which binds lovers *(Lettre à M. de Lamartine);* the contrasting joys of adoring from a distance and of voluptuous passion, both exquisitely described in *Idylle;* the theme of secret love *(Chanson de Fortunio),* and the belief that remembered love is perhaps even more real than present happiness *(Souvenir).*

Listed baldly, these topics seem stereotyped, some of them even slightly comic to our own period, which has been called the age of irony. Yet the very fact that these are still the themes which set the guitars of pop singers strumming in the twentieth century stresses that Musset touches here on one of the most universal aspects of human life. It takes a brave man and a great poet to choose such often handled material and emerge with his poetic reputation unscathed, but there is no doubt, to my mind, that Musset succeeds. His poems are scarcely ever merely the conventional "romantic" love duos of his time and are scarcely ever restricted to picture post-card prettiness. Some indeed, like *Rolla,* have powerful themes which convey a terror reinforced by strength of conviction allied to forceful, direct expression. Others have the simple charm that goes singing on in the memory, one of the tests of true poetry according to Sainte-Beuve. Always, whether the mood is of wistful charm or high seriousness, the lines have the conviction that stems from Musset's belief that love is the crux of human life and of the whole universe, love interpreted not as a brief moment of ardor but the union which can turn life into "the green pathway where, as life went on, they would smile at each other as they talked softly together" *(A George Sand,* No. III, in *Poésies post-humes).*[10]

Even the idea that love is a central force in the world is not a theory that has been banished to the attic with nineteenth-century bric-a-brac. C. Day Lewis too holds that the poet

is in the world, we may say, to bear witness to the principle of love, since love is as good a word as any for that human reaching-out of hands towards the warmth in all things, which is the source and passion of his song. Love is this to him first: but it is more; he apprehends it as a kind of necessity by which all things are bound together and in which, could the whole pattern be seen, their contradictions would appear reconciled. *(op. cit.,* pp. 36-37)

Love, then, for Musset is almost synonymous with life, or at least with life that is worth living. It is as little use to talk of having life without love as to set out to sea with no guiding star, for war with no martial music, or on a journey with no book, he writes in *Il n'est que la jeunesse (Poésies posthumes).* Yet we have seen that the word as he uses it is not confined to the feelings of a man for a woman. Throughout his poetry there recurs the note of an intense love and enjoyment inspired by life itself with all its depth and its trivia—"Sweets, the ocean, gambling, the blue of the skies,/Women, horses, laurel trees and roses" *(A M. V.H.,* in *Poésies nouvelles).*[11]

IV *Local Color and Settings*

So dense does the concentration of reflections upon life become in Musset's later poetry that it is tempting to use as a subtitle for a discussion on the *Poésies nouvelles* Musset's own line which might be translated as "What the angels of grief have taught me," and to counterbalance this by labeling the *Premières Poésies,* again borrowing the author's own words in translation, as "the interplay of imagination and poetic technique." Clearly this division would be as oversimplified and misleading as it would be convenient; we have seen that the ideas which come to full bloom in the second collection of poems were already developing in the first. On the other hand, the *Contes d'Espagne et d'Italie,* which were incorporated in the *Premières Poésies,* contain an element which Musset abandoned before he began the *Poésies nouvelles,* an element which gave free rein to his imagination in using local color in the background of his poems. By the time he came to write *Namouna,* published at the end of the *Premières Poésies* and not forming part of the *Contes d'Espagne et d'Italie,* he was ready to inform his reader that the story would make no mention of the East where the action took place. Never having visited the region would have been no handicap, he points out, mocking his fellow writers, for the Orient was so vast and so far away that a short time in the library aided by a good memory would have supplied all he needed. Who would have challenged his accuracy if he had laid on thick daubs of color—a blue-roofed town, a white mosque, all in an extravaganza spangled with silver and gold, minarets, a red horizon, and a multicolored sky? No doubt contemporary readers thought at this point of Victor Hugo's vivid *Orientales* as well as of countless lesser writers' Eastern rhapsodies.

Even when the first of the *Contes d'Espagne et d'Italie* was composed, it seems probable that Musset was amused at the overgaudy, simplified, and exaggerated guise in which foreign countries appeared in the works of the Romantic group. Exotic settings, whether of the heady South or the mysterious North, as Madame de Staël had helped to characterize them, were immensely fashionable among the reading public. It mattered little to most readers, wallowing in the visual color and excitement that Romantic vision offered them, that the image of foreign countries in the new works was a concoction, repeated *ad nauseam,* of fact mixed with the impressions and prejudices of past centuries, the anecdotes of assorted travelers, highly colored stories related by the veterans of Napoleon's armies, and popular belief—the whole strained through the sieve of the Romantics' taste in descriptive material.

The flippancy with which Musset handles his exotic themes suggests that he was too intelligent to close his eyes to the falsity and the sometimes comic exaggeration of many contemporary attempts to meet the high requirements for local color that Victor Hugo had laid down in the *Préface de Cromwell.* On the other hand, it is difficult to believe that he would have made so many excursions into this field simply for the fun of parodying other people's excesses. It seems more likely to me that, in spite of himself, he felt the undoubted fascination that dreams of countries abroad could exercise. There is certainly a great deal to be learned about his development as an artist by comparing the *Contes d'Espagne et d'Italie* with his masterly evocation of Florence in *Lorenzaccio.*

Of the two Mediterranean lands Musset dallied with in his earlier collection of poems, Spain was associated with an important event in his literary career, since his poems with Spanish themes were among the first that he read at the Arsenal evening gatherings. "The spoiled darling whom by chance they had adopted, I knocked together ballads, one to the moon, the other to two dark and jealous Andalusian eyes" *(Réponse à M. Charles Nodier).*[12] *L'Andalouse* gives a rapid sketch of an Andalusian beauty living in Barcelona and bearing the suspiciously Basque-looking name of Amaĕgui. In the course of the poem there are references to the saints of Castile and the *alcaldes* of Tolosa, capital of Guipuzcoa, so that the finished result resembles nothing so much as a Spanish topographical stew of ingredients thrown in at random. The appearance of the heroine is just as conventional and confused as the topography; Musset comments in successive lines on her pallor, "like a beautiful Autumn evening," and on her "bronzed bosom." To this are added the conventional serenades, duets, *basquiñas,* and mantillas, completing a flagrant example of a young, hot-headed Romantic, intoxicated with the hazy but colorful notions of Spain that were in the air, and flinging a haphazard selection of them together to form a poem.

In *Madrid,* Musset creates a city as fantastic as the land of Bavaria in *Fantasio.* Here, in the "white city of serenades," a series of conventional pictures flashes before us—the *paseo* or evening promenade with its procession of dainty feet; bullfights; starry nights when veiled *señoras* descend "blue stairways"; churches where lovers meet at Mass. The thread of action is of the flimsiest. A lover, achieving his objective by the fineness of his mount, by compliments on his lady's mantilla and a present of sweetmeats, visits his mistress via the window her duenna opens. It is hard to imagine greater heights of literary conventionality. The "spoilt child" of the Romantic school seems to be amusing himself throughout the poem by ridiculing the Spanish scenes of his fellow writers. The result is a world created by a fanciful, mocking imagination playing around a few conventional data.

Musset's tone changes from flippancy to the tragic in *Don Paez,* a tale of ardent love that must avenge betrayal by inflicting death. Once more the scene is a Madrid composed of all the traditional details that were part of the writer's stock-in-trade at this time. Rapidly we glimpse the Prado and its duennas, the mules, the lizard basking on a crumbling gable in the poor quarter. One phrase suffices to invoke the gaiety of Madrilenian life—"boleros, flowers, and masquerades"—and elsewhere Musset vividly portrays the city after nightfall, lapped round by the sleeping river and looking like a fairy palace as its spires assume fantastic shapes. If Musset had seen the usually muddy trickle of the Manzanares River, he would have found it far inferior to his poetic fancy, but the beauty of his language drives such thoughts from the reader's mind. After this aerial view, the camera of the narrative moves into the "Place San Bernardo" seen, inevitably, by moonlight as the monastery clock strikes. Beyond scarlet-fringed blinds we are shown a room luxurious with velvet and marble. The moonlight shines through the gray trefoils of the ogival windows for, to the French of the Romantic period, architectural Spain had to be gothic if it was not Moorish.

Far less detail is lavished on the appearance of the characters, and once more the reader must content himself with the glimpse of a *basquiña,* of the hero's cloak *à la* Hernani and golden spurs, and of the black eyebrows, white hands, and tiny feet which characterize as a matter of course the Andalusian countess who combs her long, jet-black tresses in the moonlight. Nor are there any profound character studies. It is sufficient for the action of the story that its protagonists should be violently passionate. Finally, the quota of local color is made up with a metaphor from the bullring and a sprinkling of geographical names.

These poems reveal Musset's Spain, then, as a land superficially but enthusiastically reconstructed from the bric-a-brac of literary tradition. He never allows his imagination to be chained by concern for accuracy, but releases it on flights of fancy with traces of occasional mockery. He is typical of his time in that his Spanish heroines, for instance, have to be Andalusian even though the scene may be set in a totally different region, usually Madrid in Musset's poems. A fascinating picture is conjured up of roads thronged by Andalusian countesses with raven hair, small feet, and emotions of the required temperature exporting themselves to all parts of Spain to meet French poets' need of the exotic.

Musset's enthusiasm for Italian art might lead one to expect a study in greater depth when his poems take a setting in Italy, but once again we are in a picture-postcard land, all sunshine, passion, and jealousy. Twice, in *Les Marrons du feu* and in *Venise*, "folie" is given not only as rhyming with "Italie" but as synonymous with it. "And what man is there in Italy who has not a grain of madness, who does not keep his finest days for his love affairs?" *(Venise).*[13] *Les Marrons du feu* blames the heat of the sun in Italy for the transitoriness of love there, and in *Portia* Musset describes in the bloodcurdling phrases of melodrama the "Florentine poison"—jealousy—which every man of Florence imbibes with his mother's milk; jealousy for which there is no antidote, strong enough to craze him and to destroy in a second years of love and trust. Venice is the only other region to be characterized (later on in *Portia),* with its fatal beauty and the enervating atmosphere of debauchery which Musset had the opportunity to verify during his own wretched days there.

Italy, then, equals Venice and Florence in the *Premières Poésies,* just as Spain equals Madrid and Andalusia. Wherever the setting is, we are in a land of glamorous clichés—silken ladders, serenades, churches dimly lit by torches, galloping steeds bearing beplumed gallants to their rendezvous. Yet, unlike many of his contemporaries who deal in these stereotypes, Musset does not constantly dally with description simply for its own sake. In scene viii of *Les Marrons du feu* he is content to trace the bare outlines of a backdrop: "A street that runs along by the sea. Rafael is climbing down a trellis." Such economy is rare at a time when most authors, given the scope of a foreign seascape, would wallow in an accumulation of exotic detail. On one of the few occasions when Musset pauses to paint a scene, as in Part III of *Portia,* the resulting picture is arresting. As if we were looking at a canvas by Canaletto, we see Venice at serenade time. A spring night, personified as a reveler with his feet wet with dew and his mask in his hand, sports with the dawn around St. Mark's, beneath the somber arcades. No sound disturbs the carved saints in the porticoes of the ancient palaces. The whole town is drowsing; even the waves that lap its white stairways are asleep. In the stillness and silence, the hero's boat slides into view.

La Coupe et les lèvres shows that Musset was not only aware in 1832 of just how stereotyped were the Italian clichés that he had used with gay bravado in 1830, but that he thoroughly disliked the falsity and superficiality of the contemporary idea of Italy. Here he compares her to a ragged prostitute, grown pale beneath kisses, and, continuing the image, writes of Naples handed over by its guides to crowds of tourists. Earlier, when he invited the readers of the *Contes d'Espagne et d'Italie* to quaff beakers "full of the warm South," in Keats's words, he sometimes seems to have mixed up the labels on the bottles, or indeed to have mixed the contents of the two into a hybrid wine typical of his days, half-Spanish and half-Italian. Camargo, the ferocious Italian heroine of *Les Marrons du feu,* is fond of images drawn from Spanish bullfights, and the dramatic poem ends with a speech which follows the traditional Spanish pattern for a play's closing lines, a pattern made familiar in France by Mérimée's *Théâtre de Clara Gazul* as well as by translations from the Spanish. "I have killed my friend, I have deserved eternal fire, I have stained my doublet, and I am to be sent packing, that is the moral of this play," concludes the Abbé.[14]

Since Madame de Staël had stressed the difference between the civilizations of the Mediterranean lands and Northern Europe, the one had been as popular a subject for literary dreams as the other. Like many of-his contemporaries, Musset wrote of the Swiss mountains which he had never seen at that time *(Au Yung-Frau),* and *La Coupe et les lèvres* opens with an invocation to the Tyrol, delicately colored with the icy tints of its mountain landscapes and loud in praise of the pride and love of freedom traditionally associated with mountain dwellers. Not surprisingly, since French novel readers were full of "Monk" Lewis and the English "gothic novel," when the young poet ventures into an English setting he finds himself in a melodramatic land of mists, moonlight, and macabre doings. Already in *Stances,* against a Pyrenean setting, Musset had shown that he was susceptible to the "poetry of ruins" which Chateaubriand had shown off to advantage. Here we see a deserted monastery and church, storm-torn mountains, deep-spiraling staircases, and yellowing autumn woods. The opening scene of Act IV in *La Coupe et les lèvres* plunges the reader into the same sort of sepulchral mystery, with the palace door draped in black, the coffin on its catafalque, and Frank disguised as a monk, black-robed and masked. But it is in the England of *Le Saule* that Musset makes his longest excursion into the fashionable melodrama of the day. Not surprisingly, the sketches of the countryside round the ancestral home of the Smolens contain images unusually hackneyed for Musset—the "mantle of the night" for instance—and the actual manor house is the complete horror-novel model: "Scarcely a stray light still flickers here and there in the castle. Silence. Terror. A few footsteps, a few sounds are borne on the gloomy night air. A door groans in a long passage. Tiburce is still waiting. In the darkness, are there not murderous thoughts in the seducer's mind? Everything is asleep."[15]

For good measure, the denouement takes place in a convent with the dying moans of a beautiful nineteen-year-old novice rending the air as her lover, disguised as a monk, arrives just too late to save her. There are times when one would give a great deal for insight into Musset's frame of mind when he was writing the *Contes d'Espagne et d'Italie,* so that one could know to what extent such conventional set pieces as *Le Saule* were composed flippantly, to poke the finger of fun at contemporary extravagances in literature. Perhaps, even in such an extreme case, he was half in love with the thrill of the new, fashionable themes. Whether or not he wrote most of the poem with his tongue in his cheek, at the melodramatic height of the convent sequence there are stanzas such as that beginning "Do you know what a young girl's heart is?" which already show the perceptive seriousness with which he could analyze feelings.

During the same period when he was taking these flights into exotic distance, Musset could also write a refreshingly realistic sonnet full of affection for Paris in the winter, and in *Mardoche* glimpses flash past the reader's eye of fashionable Paris with its shops and entertainments, the costumes and carriages of its dandies, and the *grisette,* "trotting along like a partridge" and making eyes with deadly effect. By the time the last poems included in the *Premières Poésies* were being written, the conventional shapes of contemporary exoticism had almost disappeared from Musset's equipment, whether used in jest or not. *A quoi rêvent les jeunes filles* takes place, with a fine disregard for Victor Hugo's insistence on the importance of characteristic setting, "où l'on voudra" ("wherever you will"), and the twin heroines' looks and dress are left to the reader's imagination in the same way. Only occasionally are we given any specific detail, such as the shepherdess costumes of Ninon and Ninette in scene vii of Act II. From now on, most of his settings have a nebulous poetry, like that of *Fantasio,* which, while heightening the impression made by the characters as the Romantics wished, never places before the reader a weighty array of detail. This change of technique was the bridge leading to *Lorenzaccio* where Musset fused the same unobtrusive poetic quality with a powerful evocation of place and time which achieves all that the advocates of local color desired without falling into any of their errors of distortion.

By the time the *Poésies nouvelles* were composed, exotic themes had almost disappeared from Musset's poetry. In the poem greeting Paul on his return from Italy, the country is characterized lightly and briefly, although affectionately, as the place "where macaroni and music were born." In this volume there is an occasional excursion to a vivid landscape belonging to the past, as in the scene with figures which takes us to Classical Greece in the first stanza of *Rolla,* but far more often these poems of Musset's maturity remain in his everyday world, against a background of Paris or the French countryside, again a gentle countryside reminiscent of the Ile-de-France. If overlavish description had never marred even Musset's early poetry, now, in the later collection, he is increasingly sparing with his word-pictures. When, in the opening lines of canto v, Rolla gazes out of his window to see the sun rising over Paris, many of Musset's contemporaries would have inserted a solid wedge of highly colored description of the day dawning over the city. All that Musset sketches in for us are the heavy carts beginning to trundle along the streets below; a straggling group of street singers softly singing one of those old ballads which he says are all the more nostalgic for their reminders of the innocence of childhood. The only touch of color comes from the clouds, "rent in long rivers of blood," which make Musset think of Christ's agony. There is no detail which does not help to heighten the atmosphere and underline the state of the hero's mind.

Economy of description does not mean lack of visual appeal or lack of evocative power. Some scenes in the *Poésies nouvelles* convey the swarming horror of a Goya painting, for instance the depiction of Paris in the debauchery of carnival time in *Lettre à M. de Lamartine.* There are other scenes as enchanting and as lyrically evoked as any in French verse, scenes which repay visit after visit from the reader to whom they appeal. For some it may be the rhapsodic spring evening of *La Nuit de mai;* for others, the more muted forest scenery of *Souvenir.*

V   *The Figures Who People Musset's Poetry*

Exquisite scene painter as Musset may be, his landscapes rarely lack figures, and it is almost always the figures who predominate over their setting. Indeed, his dramatic gifts shine through so clearly in much of his poetry that sometimes the reader has to keep reminding himself that a particular work is in fact classified as a poem and not as part of Musset's "armchair theater."

When one comes to look at the types of character portrayed in the *Premières Poésies* and the *Poésies nouvelles,* it is to find a development following the same pattern as in his use of local color. In the first collection of poems nearly all the main figures fall into one of two clear-cut and stereotyped groups, the Romantic hero and the Romantic heroine. The cardboard models used countless times by countless authors during this period did permit slight variations, and as far as the hero is concerned, Musset favors, in preference to the languishing weeping-willow variety, the more dynamic young man met in versions of the Don Juan story and in Byron's poems, although it must be remembered that Musset denies any imitation of Byron. Rafael in *Les Marrons du feu,* casually killing an old innkeeper by throwing a bottle at his head, is a nineteenth-century delinquent who shows a callousness rare in Musset's later works but common enough in the melodrama of the day. The taciturn young lover in *Le Saule* has a gaze that is hard and severe, capable of a lightning flash that pierces straight to Georgette's heart. This, lightly sketched in, is the "fatal man" whose powers were to pass later in the century to the better known *femme fatale*—Carmen and her tribe.

Dalti, the hero of *Portia,* like Tiburce in *Le Saule,* is enveloped in mystery in the true Romantic fashion, until at last he reveals to his mistress a story which is equally typical of the day. Like Hugo's Ruy Blas, he has spent his early years in poverty, educated but a fisherman, wandering barefoot at night by the magnificent palaces of the rich, a social misfit like so many contemporary heroes. As with many other Romantic characters too, it is chance that shapes his life, in his case the luck of the gaming table.

Mardoche and the two types of Don Juan Musset analyzes in *Namouna* are worth studying as examples of this same stereotyped Romantic hero, but perhaps the most detailed portrait in the *Premières Poésies* is that of Frank in *La Coupe et les lèvres.* His first appearance characterizes him as proud, solitary, unfortunate, scornful, and desperate; all these traits reaching the point of exaggeration, so that the scene ends with his setting fire to his cottage, his only possession. In the next act, his role is that of the young lover devoured physically and mentally by passion, yet at the same time cynical and insulting, as Musset himself could be. In later scenes, despite his successes, we see him with the "pallor of death on his brow," wrapped in self-torturing introspection that leads him to attend his own faked funeral in an attempt to discover the real value put on his life by others. This incident ends with a long soliloquy—a device rare in Musset's work—in which Frank gives vent to many of the troubles that caused anguish to the Romantic generation. He is suicidal and unable to believe in an afterlife; he is frantic at having left no permanent mark on this world and is willing to indulge in evil if this will cause him to be remembered. Consumed by hatred, at the same time he is full of a desperate hunger for life, which yet disgusts him because of the lack of belief and the spirit of excessive analysis which have sucked all vitality from his day and age, leaving the world a neatly ordered cemetery. Why has man been given an ardent thirst for the ideal, asks Frank in an echo of young Musset's letter to Paul Foucher, if there is nothing to assuage it?

Rafael, Dalti, Mardoche, Tiburce, Frank—all these characters, then, are variations on the international theme of the Romantic hero, the theme that is illustrated in Manfred and Werther, in Hernani and Chatterton, in a new interpretation of Don Juan as an idealistic searcher after elusive perfection. This group of Musset's characters is too busy alternately striking a pose and taking part in rapid action to present much depth of personality, but in spite of their exaggeration most of them have a lifelike quality which often eludes other French Romantic heroes. Frank especially, with his defiant questioning of life, rises from time to time above the surrounding melodrama to speak words which have the ring of truth.

Unlike Musset's theater, where we shall find women occupying at least as important roles as men, the *Contes d'Espagne et d'Italie* contain no portrait of the Romantic heroine as detailed as that of Frank. Those heroines who appear on stage in these dramatic poems are even more highly colored than their male partners, and it is interesting to see that most of them belong to the category of the "black" Romantic heroine—the vampirish, satanic seducer who inevitably leads men to their downfall. Camargo in *Les Marrons du feu,* Mariette and her murderess in *Octave,* and Belcolore in *La Coupe et les lèvres* form a mounting crescendo of destructive fury. Camargo, whose imagery taken from bullfighting we mentioned, has herself all the violence of the bullring; her love, she says, is a blade of steel. As for Mariette, she was a Messalina who "opened her rapacious arms to change her frail favorites into old men and, spreading death beneath her hectic kisses, drank in avidly the elements she dearly loved, gold and blood." Like Gautier's Cleopatra, Belcolore is the very type of the *femme fatale;* "siren and prostitute, foulness personified; the machine invented to cut man open and drink his blood; the millstone of degradation. What a strange atmosphere one breathes around her! She drains men's strength, she destroys them, and is all the fairer for it. Two angels of devastation walk at her side; both are beguiling and cruel—death, and voluptuous pleasure."[16] Musset invested Belcolore with the type of looks he himself was susceptible to, with "two great eyes as black as Hades" which bring George Sand to mind.

Amid all this fatal sultriness, it is almost a relief to find an example, although equally stereotyped, of the other kind of Romantic heroine. Georgina Smolen, the victim of love in *Le Saule,* is as angelic, as golden-haired, blue-eyed, chaste, and innocent as any idealized vision of woman by a Romantic author. The women who people the *Comédies et Proverbes* are so different from these stock characters, the subtlety, delicacy, and depth of their natures form such a commonplace of criticism, that a study of the heroines of the *Contes d'Espagne et d'Italie* and of *La Coupe et les lèvres* serves as a reminder that Musset could and did produce mere replicas of the types fashionable in contemporary literature at the beginning of his literary career. Our admiration for his later creations, for Camille and Marianne, can only grow by comparison.

Moving like a shadowy figure among these Romantic heroes and heroines and the lesser characters who surround them, the author himself sometimes appears to the reader. In stanza xx of *Namouna*, Musset flatly denies that he has depicted himself in Hassan. Perhaps, he would have denied too that in *Les Marrons du feu* Rafael's boredom, debauchery, melancholy, and fantasy are similar to his own, or that when the coin spun onto its other side, he could be very like the witty, flippant, roisterous *bon vivant* presented by this same character in scene iii. Yet it is impossible not to hear Musset himself speaking when Frank describes bitterly the power of vice, so strong that a man's first dalliance with it leaves a stain which oceans of water cannot wash away, or when the poem called *Les Vœux stériles* tells how physical suffering is always recognized by others, but how a man close to death through mental anguish cannot expect even his intimate friends to understand his plight. Having written these words, Musset sets his seal on them as a personal confession by admitting that tears had sprung to his eyes as he composed the poem.

One of the most striking developments that can be traced in Musset's poetry is that, whereas in the *Premières Poésies* he moves like a puppet master behind his figures, appearing only briefly, in the *Poésies nouvelles* the list of dramatis personae is reduced very largely to Musset himself and to the women he loved. From a world comparatively external to him, his poetry moves to a world far more intimate, personal, and real. It is true that other figures appear on the sidelines and that the mood is not restricted to the intensity of love themes. There are the two grotesques Dupont and Durand, for instance, two failures of the Romantic group, with their comic appearance and ways, who allow Musset to poke fun at contemporary trends. Nor has the Romantic hero disappeared, since Rolla, one of the best known of Musset's representatives of this type, is included in the *Poésies nouvelles.*

Far more often, however, in this volume Musset dispenses with the masks of fiction and appears directly before his reader. He tells of the gaiety of his Arsenal days *(Réponse à M. Charles Nodier)*, of his drinking *(A Mme Jaubert)*, of artists' attempts to paint him *(Sur mes portraits)*, and in 1845 of his premonitions of death *(L'Heure de ma mort)*. (The last three poems mentioned were published posthumously but belong to the same period as those published in *Poésies nouvelles.)* The reader discovers all manner of facets of Musset's nature, such as the emotional dependence on his brother, which can be seen in *A mon frère, revenant d'Italie;* but generally it is the central problems, beliefs, and griefs of his life that raise his emotions to the white heat needed to produce poetry. *La Nuit de décembre* conveys the full force of the loneliness, weariness, and boredom that so often weighed down his spirits, while *La Nuit d'octobre* and many another poem relate the sufferings caused by disappointments in love and by the irrecoverable loss of his innocence. The *Lettre à M. de Lamartine* contains one line which, perhaps even better than more widely known poems such as *Tristesse,* brings awareness of the depth of wretchedness which Musset knew: "Seul, je me suis assis dans la nuit de mon cœur."[17]

Yet even when poems deal with incidents as heartbreaking for Musset as the end of his relationship with George Sand, he rarely indulges in the excessive, lachrymose wallowing in grief which is often associated with the Romantics. Even when he relates, in the poem addressed to his brother on his return from Italy, what a shattering change in his nature his own visit to Italy had brought about, he handles his theme with a light touch, and *Souvenir,* that poem dedicated above all others to his memories of past happiness with George, has a triumphant, thankful tone. "Proudly lies this forest in its peaceful beauty, and my heart too is proud."[18] The sadness of *La Nuit d'octobre* ends with a resolve to banish hatred for the injury done him and find rebirth in renewed gaiety. Other verses, like the sonnet dedicated in 1838 to Alfred Tattet, are full of an unqualified love of life that one sometimes forgets when thinking of Musset. Above all he shows himself again, as one would expect, to be the high priest of love, before which neither life nor death are of any importance and against which no suffering must be allowed to close the heart. "Strip away before all eyes the pride that is devouring you, heart swollen with bitterness and who thought yourself closed. Love, and you will be born again; turn yourself into a flower to burst into bloom. When man has suffered, he must suffer again; he must go on loving for ever, when one love is over."[19]

Many poets have drawn on their own experience to feed their poetry, but few can have analyzed their own mental ills with the perception which makes Musset his own psychoanalyst in the posthumously published *Stances.* Yet one feels oneself to be in the presence not of a morbid Narcissus but of a man expressing and intelligently trying to come to grips with the difficulties in his life.

VI *Feminine Figures*

When one turns one's attention to the feminine roles in the *Poésies nouvelles* it is to find the sometimes caricatural heroines of the *Premières Poésies* replaced by a very few, mostly real, figures, by La Malibran, Lucie, Princess Belgiojoso, and above all by George Sand who seems to be at the source of so many of these later poems even when they do not speak of her openly. When Musset does mention her name directly, the resulting poetry is sometimes as effective as the tragic and simple tones of *Souvenir.* Here he calls her "my only love, who will always be dearest to me," obviously not sharing some critics' opinions of her relative importance among his mistresses. The third posthumous poem called *A George Sand* is perhaps the best example of these haunting love poems, full of the power of true feeling and the freshness of personal experience.

Among the handful of fictitious women, the waxlike figure of Georgina Smolen is replaced by the young heroine of *Rolla,* just as idealized but far more alive and obviously meaning far more to Musset as an example of the endangered innocence of youth. The tenderness with which he portrays Marie is thrown into relief by the harshness of the Goya-like picture of bedraggled prostitutes who appear for a second in the half-open door. Not all the women depicted in the *Poésies nouvelles* belong to this world of high drama, and for light relief there is the gaiety, good sense, and courage of Mimi Pinson, the blonde *grisette* with her one dress.

VII *Language, Technique, and Versification*

Scarcely ever, unless he happens to be a specialist in prosody, is the reader's attention diverted from the substance of Musset's poetry to its form, and this unobtrusiveness is a tribute to the skill which fuses the two together. Carelessness in fulfilling technical requirements is the usual defect with which Musset the poet is charged, but it is more likely to be sudden admiration for some striking image, vivid descriptive passage, or captivating rhythm that occasionally stops the general reader in his tracks than disapproval for some academic insufficiency of rhyme.

It is surprising how seldom, even in the *Premières Poésies,* one finds examples of typically Romantic devices. Perhaps the characteristic that brings some of these poems closest to the mass of contemporary works is the hint of melodrama that creeps in from time to time. The hero of *Le Saule* sails away in the dead of night, grief-stricken, solitary, singing a mysterious dirge, swooning repeatedly with weakness as his blood drips from the wound hidden beneath his cloak. *La Coupe et les lèvres* too has moments which belong to the world of the horror novel, especially in the last scene when the hero and heroine, only an hour before their wedding, are disturbed by a wild-eyed apparition staring at them through the window, an apparition who turns out to be Belcolore, about to wreak her vengeance by stabbing the bride-to-be through the heart with her stiletto.

One of the passages most likely to make twentieth-century readers guffaw instead of shudder occurs in *Portia.* The two young lovers are together on a moonlit night when the lamp suddenly goes out. When Portia relights it, " 'Heaven and earth, Dalti! There are three of us here,' she said. 'Three,' repeated close by them a voice which echoed in the far-away castle vaults. Motionless, hidden in the folds of a cloak, like an ancient statue in a doorway, Onorio loomed before their startled gaze."[20] No doubt Musset too was amused as he wrote these lines, but many authors of his day were serving up such fare, even more highly seasoned, in deadly seriousness. Yet often when a plot offers a chance, which such writers would have seized, to embroider the text with lurid detail, Musset handles the incident with skillful but sober economy. *Don Paez,* for instance, ends with the two lovers dying violent deaths, but there is none of the gory, long-drawn-out description which the fashion of the day delighted in.

By the time most of the *Poésies nouvelles* came into being, Musset had finished with such hackneyed melodrama and, although almost every line shows that he is a poet of the Romantic period, it is rare for him to use Romantic clichés. Even when he chooses a theme as typically Romantic as that of his elegy *Lucie* and treats it in a typically lyrical way, the overriding impression, for me at least, is touchingly fresh. Yet even Musset's admirers must recognize that there are readers of other tastes who find in *Lucie* an oversweetness which characterizes for them the qualities that they find nauseating in Romantic writings.

When one focuses one's attention on imagery, the discretion and restraint with which Musset used it, after he had had his fling with the famous dot over the "i" in *Ballade à la lune,* is no surprise, but analysis shows a surprising lack of conventional images and the even more surprising fact that a very high proportion of the most striking metaphors and similes are of one particular type. Almost all of them bring to life inanimate objects or abstractions. Usually the animating image transforms the object described into human shape, although in *Don Paez* poison is very effectively compared to a cat cruelly 'playing with its prey. A few lines earlier, the sorceress's hovel is personified in an unusual way as the crouching form of an old spinning woman. We have already seen how, similarly, a spring night in Venice turns enchantingly in canto iii of *Portia* into a reveler, his feet in the dew, his mask in his hand, sporting with the morning.

This is one characteristic of the *Premières Poésies* which is just as marked in the *Poésies nouvelles,* where the nineteenth century is personified as Lazarus, and earth as a despairing woman weary of giving birth and finding rest in barrenness. These images occur in *Rolla* and here too the hero's passions are portrayed as a horde of drunken travelers wreaking havoc in an inn. The figures in these images do not usually appear more than once except for the prostitute, a repetition which underlines what we already know of Musset's concern for her. In general, though, the significance of the predominant animating images is surely the way in which they stress the essentially dramatic nature of Musset's creative gifts, objects and abstractions which he describes tending to take on life and a role of their own. This is not to say that purely pictorial images are unknown in the two volumes; *Rolla,* for instance, brings before the reader a desert scene which could rival those of Leconte de Lisle for vividness.

The born dramatist is seen clearly too in the naturalness of the frequent passages of dialogue. Most of his great plays may be in prose, but in his poems Musset proves that conversation in verse can have the true ring of everyday speech, the poetic form serving to heighten the desired effect without bringing artificiality in its train. This is what Hugo had preached in the *Préface de Cromwell* when he recommended verse as the medium for the Romantic drama, and certainly dramatic poems such as *Don Paez* show that, in the right hands, his recommendation was justified. Musset's passages of dialogue have not the compact brilliance and beauty of Hugo's, but they have a suppleness that enables him to mold them exactly to the rhythms of speech. In the barrack room in *Don Paez* a soldier makes himself heard above the din, issuing a challenge which, in the first two lines of verse especially, bends the alexandrine to the irregularity of the pattern of casual speech.

L'un d'eux: "Messieurs, dit-il, vous êtes gens du roi,
Braves gens, cavaliers volontaires.—Bon.—Moi,
Je vous déclare ici trois fois gredin et traître,
Celui qui ne va pas proclamer, reconnaître,
Que les plus belles mains qu'en ce chien de pays
On puisse voir encor de Burgos à Cadix,
Sont celles de doña Cazales de Séville,
Laquelle est ma maîtresse, au dire de la ville!"[21]

The following exchange between Don Paez and his rival has the flashing rapidity of their blades when they leave words for weapons. In a completely different setting, among the frills and furbelows of *A quoi rêvent les jeunes filles,* Ninon's first monologue is astonishing for the way it captures and reproduces, with the same suppleness, the stream of inconsequential thoughts that can pass through a young girl's head in any century. Brawling soldiery and daydreaming girls mingle their voices with all the others found in this poetry and with an occasional medieval note when Musset gives language an archaic look to add to the charm of a poem. In *Madame la Marquise* we find the phrase "fors notre amour," and the next to the last stanza turns old legal forms of speech into romance.

Pour ce, madame la marquise,
Dès qu'à la ville il fera noir,
De par le roi sera requise
De venir en notre manoir.

At the other end of the scale, Rafaël must have shocked the first readers of *Les Marrons du feu* with his description of himself in the language of a thoroughly un-Classical hero as "salé comme un hareng" as he emerges dripping from the sea in the opening scene.

Language in Musset's hands is a chameleon, taking on the accent of any character and of different periods, now charmingly antiquated, now brashly modern, and he is adept too at reproducing the rhythm of music—of the barcarolle in *Venise* and the bolero in the posthumous poem of that name. In a less specific way there are several songs— *Chanson de Barberine, Chanson de Fortunio,* the *chanson* beginning "J'ai dit à mon cœur, à mon faible cœur" with the echo effect of its repeated phrases, and the other which starts with the line "A Saint-Blaise, à la Zuecca"—which are typical of the way in which Musset's verses fulfil Sainte-Beuve's requirements that lines of poetry should be "easy on the memory and on the ear."

As with imagery and style in general, versification plays the role of contributing effectively to the impression made by the poem, and yet remaining as unobtrusive as possible. This is true except in some comparatively early works such as *Mardoche,* where the carrying on of a sentence from the last line of a stanza to the first line of the next seems intended to shock the first readers, nurtured in Classicism, just as Hugo electrified the audience on the first night of *Hernani* with his "... escalier/Dérobé...."

The first poem Musset ever published *(Un Rêve,* included by Van Tieghem in the section of his edition entitled "Poésies non recueillies par Musset") shows that even at eighteen he was a skilled enough versifier to supply with apparent ease the "rich rhymes" that pleased the Romantics, and fifteen years later in *Réponse à M. Charles Nodier* he was lightheartedly juggling with rhymes to add to the gaiety of most of the poem. Musset's jibes at the careful rhyming of the "carpenter-poets" whom he mentions in the dedication to *La Coupe et les lèvres* and his insistence that freedom was better than systems sometimes make one forget his technical skill in rhyming; and it is just as easy to overlook the effectiveness with which he handles the larger component parts of verse. He has after all been called a master of the difficult sonnet form, in which few of his contemporaries excelled (See J. Suberville, *Histoire et théorie de la versification française,* 2nd edition, Paris: Editions de l'Ecole, n.d., p. 229). Romantic poetry tends to prefer longer and more exotic stanza structure, but Musset has the conciseness in making his point and the ability to construct which make his sonnets as exquisite as Chopin's preludes. In longer poems, especially in the *Nuits,* varying stanza forms represent different voices and moods with a skill which again shows poetic and dramatic gifts working together.

Indeed, the descriptive technique in early poems such as *Don Paez* is often so dramatic that the examination question which asks students to judge whether *Lorenzaccio* would make a good movie could be applied here on a smaller scale. In canto ii one can imagine the camera first following Don Paez as he walks the ramparts, his cigar glowing in the dark, then closing to give shots of the grouped soldiers. The sound effects are all indicated, and the scene which might have been static is in fact full of movement: one man in his cups is telling a bawdy story; another props his elbow on the table as he croons under his breath; one examines his dice, grinding his teeth with suspicion, while a braggart makes play with his beplumed hat and another, his beard stained with the red wine, unsteadily pours himself another drink and toasts the king's health. All the while a dwindling candle quivers with each fist-blow on the table.

In *La Coupe et les lèvres* Musset tries out a technique from the Classical Greek theater, using a chorus for such purposes as describing the battle which took place before the start of Act III, and later in the same scene introducing two choruses—one of the people and one of knights—to acclaim the victorious hero. This device was to bring originality, humor, and poetry to *On ne badine pas avec l'amour.* Bathos and anticlimax too were tricks of the trade of poets such as Pope and Byron, and the last three stanzas of *Mardoche* prove that Musset was already adept at using them. When Mardoche and Rosine are surprised by her husband, we are told in heroic language to what lengths the hero was ready to go to save the queen of his heart from disgrace. Too bad that his gallant feat of leaping from the window is foiled by a common sprained ankle. Meanwhile, the lady in distress "had the disappointed look that a parakeet wears when he has been teasingly tossed a bean wrapped in blotting-paper to disguise it as a sugared almond." Like the heroine of *Le Saule,* she is packed off to a convent, but no tragic consequences are related; and as for the hero, far from sailing out to meet his death from self-inflicted wounds, after six months he finds a new love.

It must not be forgotten that Musset, when he wished, could also vie with his contemporaries in verbal landscape painting, as the panorama he depicts in *Venise* shows. Indeed one of the attractions of his poetry lies in its variety of style, technique, and mood. Whereas some poets seem to have one particular prevailing tonal color, so that Gautier can talk in his *Histoire du romantisme* of the soft, silvery grays and opal tints of Vigny's work, Musset's readers find a whole spectrum of changing colors. Perhaps in the *Premières Poésies* it is the flippant, mocking Musset who appears more often than any other, sometimes cynical, sometimes bawdy; but we also see him in moments of tenderness, matching delicacy of sentiment with charm of expression. The *Poésies nouvelles* offer an even wider range. Opening with the strength and starkness of the poet's despair in the first part of *Rolla,* it continues with the cynicism of the first stanza in *A la Malibran;* the simplicity and objectiveness of the storytelling in *Silvia;* the biting, martial tone of *Le Rhin allemand* which reveals a little-known side of Musset's nature; the passionate feeling and nostalgia of the *Nuits;* and the witty gallantry and tenderness of so many of the poems. *Le Mie Prigioni* typifies these changing moods, for after its lighthearted beginning the poet is finally overwhelmed with emotion.

Most of these moods are well known to readers of Musset, but the fame of some of the poems written in a tragic and ardent vein perhaps makes one forget how often and how successfully he writes comic verse, poking fun at the Versailles court in *Sur trois marches de marbre rose* and composing one delicious piece called *L'Anglaise en diligence (Poésies posthumes)* where he skillfully reproduces the bouncing of the coach and caricatures its occupants. "What astounds me is that the Englishman can travel as far as Peru without ever opening his mouth except to eat or drink."

VIII *Musset's Greatness as a Poet*

If I have pointed out ways in which Musset's dramatic gifts sometimes shine through his poetry, this does not mean that the two volumes of his verse are appendages to his theater. If he was a born dramatist, he was also a born poet and to my mind it would be difficult to differentiate between his poetry and plays in order of quality. During recent years it has been unfashionable, in some British universities at least, to award more than a grudging respect to Romantic poets. Obviously Romantic literature in any language, rocketing between heights of elation and the abyss of despair, is only too easy to guy if the commentator has a mind to do so, and Musset's poetry is no exception, especially if an impression of him is formed just from some of the more impassioned "purple passages" in anthologies. Yet it is my conviction that much of his verse, particularly in the *Poésies nouvelles,* measures up to any canons of poetic greatness.

In this chapter I have tried to analyze some of the reasons that support this opinion—to show that, as in Vigny's poetry, there is here a real concern for the problems of human existence; that, after flirting with the more flamboyant themes and stylistic devices of Romanticism, Musset's poetry generally discarded these for simplicity and the essential realities of human life; that he possessed technical poetic skills which are forgotten when comments are made merely on his occasional carelessness and his scorn for mere prosodic correctness. I have tried to show too that he had that reverence for the moment of poetic creation, for the coming of inspiration, which many poets seem to share for the "White Goddess," whether they describe her symbolically or prosaically.

However, there comes a moment in musical appreciation when melody, harmony, form, and orchestration have all been analyzed and the analyst must invite his audience simply to listen to the music. This must surely happen with poetry too, and so we have returned to the starting point of this chapter, with the poet turned critic who maintained that the recognition of great poetry was as instinctive as the housewife's "nose" for sound goods. The excerpts which might be chosen to illustrate the worth of Musset's poetry would certainly change with each selector, and there is great variety to be drawn on. Apart from the despairing splendor of stanzas from the introduction to *Rolla,* which has already been mentioned, and the intimate, fireside charm of the introduction to *Silvia,* there is the exquisite passage from Act I, scene iii of *A quoi rêvent les jeunes filles* where the twins describe their awakening feelings; the eloquent simplicity, tortured and then triumphant, of the last stanzas of *Souvenir;* and the strength of the credo with its hammered-out refrain, "Your soul is immortal," which ends the *Lettre à M. de Lamartine,* strong as certain passages from Chopin whose forcefulness has been forgotten as often as Musset's.

It would be a cliché of clichés to say that the common denominator of most of the haunting passages is that they express in a masterly way feelings that the majority of men experience, but it would nevertheless be true. Especially when he speaks as a man in love, Musset brings the enchantment of the great artist to situations and emotions which the writer of lyrics for "pop" songs is still using to voice what is close to the heart of the public. After all, "Margot" was for Musset the supreme arbiter of taste.

CHAPTER 4

An Armchair Theater

I *Introduction*

I F the *Premières Poésies* and the *Poésies nouvelles* had somehow
been lost to posterity, French literature would have been bereft of
some of its crop of true poetry. Yet if one were forced to weigh
this poetry against the *Comédies et Proverbes,* I think it would be in
favor of the plays that the scales of literary greatness would tip,
however slightly. No doubt many readers would reach the opposite
conclusion, but surely few could deny that, whereas Musset stands as
one of a number of great Romantic poets, his dramatic gifts place him
alone at the very pinnacle of the Romantic theater. It is true that
Victor Hugo's plays are magnificent in spectacle and poetry, but so too
are Musset's, and in addition almost every scene he wrote reveals his
innate dramatic skills.

Cyril Connolly in his *Enemies of Promise* (London, 1938) says that
it is authors with little to tell of human nature who indulge most in
adorning their writings with purple patches, and this belief points to
one of the main differences between Musset and the majority of
dramatists of his day. It was a time when the stage was either
vivid—sometimes lurid—with the firework displays of exotic local color,
or else plunged in the melodramatic gloom of caves, tombs, or cloisters
complete with ghosts, depraved monks, and all the other trappings of
fashionable horror; when Romantic heroes and heroines gave vent to
their often stereotyped feelings in long outpourings of verse or poetic
prose; when, in fact, the dramatist more often relied on would-be
splendor of stage setting and language and melodramatic assaults on the
spectators' emotions than on penetrating studies of the characters.
Immediately exceptions, such as Vigny's stark play *Chatterton,* come to
mind, but even so it is Musset who, more than any other writer for the
stage, carries on through his span of the nineteenth century the
Classical French tradition of a theater whose main source of continuing

life is its concentration on men's minds and motives. This he does while remaining in some ways the ultra-Romantic of the Romantic dramatists, so that we are confronted with such paradoxes as *Lorenzaccio,* the play which comes closest to realizing the visions of the *Préface de Cromwell,* Hugo's manifesto, and yet whose technique often recalls Racine. A glance at Parisian billboards in our day shows that the recipe for literary survival worked as well for Musset as for the great seventeenth-century dramatists.

It is ironic that the theater debut of the man later acclaimed as the greatest playwright of his period was one of the most searing experiences that could have been suffered by a fledgling writer. It will be remembered that the first night of Musset's *La Nuit vénitienne* was as notorious a disaster as the first night of Hugo's *Hernani* was a celebrated if stormy success. This was a time when Classical diehards and partisans of the new Romanticism were turning theaters into arenas as turbulent as any twentieth-century sports stadium, and the warring factions in the audience might well have refused Musset's first play a proper hearing even without its weaknesses and without the ludicrous accidents of the stuck curtain and the wet paint, which turned the spectators into a cackling, braying mob who filled the house with a continuous uproar. To have his opening night ruined because of the literary quarrels of the time, as Vigny's was when his Desdemona dared to use such an everyday word as "handkerchief" in *Le More de Venise,* would have at least left Musset with his pride intact, but laughter is well known to be a far more deadly weapon than abuse.

In emotional coinage it was a high price to pay for the benefits most of his plays reaped from being written for staging in the imaginations of armchair readers, and from being set free from the technical restrictions of the contemporary theater whose menagerie-like spectators Musset had sworn he would never confront again. He kept his promise by not writing specifically for the theater until 1849, when *Louison* was presented at the Comédie-Française. The audience was justifiably lukewarm in its reception of the play, and the paradox remains true that the best dramas of the most skillful of the Romantic playwrights were conceived in isolation from the stage, to be read and not to be acted.

II *Settings*

It is strange too that these plays, which had no physical embodiment on the stage for some time after their creation and which have none of the long, minutely detailed instructions about costume and stage setting which preface each act of Hugo's plays, nevertheless leave as vivid a visual impression on the imagination as any other work in an age which reinstated spectacle as an integral part of the drama. The *Préface de Cromwell* had advocated that the dramatist should mirror reality not only in character portrayal but also in a faithful re-creation of the place and the moment in time to which the action of the play belonged. The theater was no longer to be "a bare board and a passion" or "a conversation beneath a chandelier" as in Classical times, but neither was local color intended to run riot in a profusion of mere superficial decoration. Hugo, stage manager almost as much as dramatist, believed that the place where an incident took place retained the indelible imprint of the event, and that on the other hand the setting contributed to the peculiar individuality of that event; the perfect play, then, should be permeated with its setting.

When Hugo came to put his theories into practice, spectacle sometimes seemed to dominate both plot and characters, but this can never be said of Musset. Even in the earliest plays there is the greatest economy in filling in background detail, and the few details that are given have a definite role to play in the development of the plot or in illustrating the characters. In *André del Sarto,* for instance, where one might have found lyrical descriptions of Florence, indications of setting are rare, and each has its precise dramatic function. In Act I, scene i, Damien's comment that the sun is rising and Cordiani's "Come, let us be off; the courtyard is beginning to fill with people, and it is time for the academy to open" both use words, much as Shakespeare does, to replace stage lighting or crowds of actors, which have their existence in the imagination alone. During the same scene Cordiani fills in for the reader the wider background of the city beyond the walls of André's garden. "I am thinking of Florence stirring from its sleep, of its promenades, the people passing by."

In *Les Caprices de Marianne,* Musset allows us the merest glimpse of the characters' appearance, and even when we learn in Act I, scene i that Octave is in carnival costume, his cheeks thickly rouged, and that Coelio is pale and enveloped in a black cloak, these indications serve as symbols of the two men's personalities and the contrast between them. In the same way the chorus at the opening of *On ne badine pas avec l'amour* uses landscape to establish what type of persons Blazius and Dame Pluche are. Blazius, it says, arrives "at the time of the grape harvest, like an ancient amphora," while Dame Pluche comes like fever "with the wind which turns the woods yellow. . . . Our cornfields are as parched as your bones."

As well as using brief references to background scenery both to symbolize a character and contribute to the setting in the reader's imagination, Musset shows his dramatic skill in scene ix of Act IV in *Lorenzaccio* by interpolating an unexpected vignette of an idyllic country landscape into the midst of Lorenzo's feverish preparations for murder. Suddenly, remembering how he once saw Louise Strozzi sewing in the shade of a chestnut tree, he thinks of the peace and the view at Cafaggiuolo; of Jeannette, the concierge's daughter, chasing the goats away from the clean clothes spread on the grass to dry. At first sight there seems no justification for this lyrical reminiscence except its own charm, but, set in the monologue of almost demented feverishness, its idealized peacefulness serves admirably to heighten by contrast the frenzy and violent atmosphere of the scene.

All these fragments of scene painting are examples of *décor parlé*, of background sketched in by information given in the dialogue, and it is rare for Musset to use any other method. His instructions at the beginning of scenes are brief and colorless in the extreme. Act II, scene iii of *On ne badine pas avec l'amour* is to take place in "a field in front of a cottage"; scene v in the same act is to be "a fountain in a wood." It is the characters who, with their speeches, build up for us a vivid picture around these sparse indications. Scarcely has Perdican begun to speak in Act II, scene v before his words depict Camille sitting among the daisies by the fountain, reflected in its waters. For a theater where readers must be their own scene painters, this technique of weaving threads of the backcloth into the fabric of the dialogue itself is far more effective than the orthodox method of concentrating all the information in a solid wedge at the outset of each scene or act. In just this way Shakespeare compensated for the lack of stage scenery and at the same time gave literature such lines as "How sweet the moonlight sleeps upon this bank" *(The Merchant of Venice,* Act V, scene i). With his usual restraint, Musset never overloads the dialogue with pictorial detail, and yet often a whole play seems permeated with the poetry of its setting.

Scarcely ever do any of these settings fall into one of the cliché-ridden categories which Romantic dramatists reproduced ad nauseam. In *La Nuit vénitienne,* it is true, the curtain rises on a stereotyped scene—night in Venice with a gondola for the hero and a balcony for the heroine—but Musset does not daub the following scenes with local color. Perhaps the only play whose background is comic in its exaggerated Romanticism is the very early one, *La Quittance du Diable,* which was written in 1830 and prepared for performance at the Théâtre des Nouveautés but never reached its first night. At that date its theme, an imitation of Walter Scott, was the height of literary fashion, but nowadays the ruined chapel, the storm, the cemetery with its capering skeletons and the stranger enveloped in his cloak, all part of the paraphernalia of the horror novel and the melodrama, would be more likely to make an audience laugh than shudder.

Later plays remind us that Musset shared the passion his period felt for Italy, but in such plays as *André del Sarto* and *Les Caprices de Marianne* there is none of the lighthearted exaggeration of the *Premières Poésies.* In the latter play, Musset seems to establish both the picture and the atmosphere of an Italian town, although he does this with such rapid and spaced brush strokes that other readers disagree, finding scarcely any local color until Octave's lines in the last scene: "Farewell, gaiety of my youth; the madcap pranks, the merry free life at the foot of Vesuvius! Farewell to the roistering dinners, the long talks at evening, the serenades beneath golden balconies! Farewell, Naples and its women, the masquerades by torchlight, the leisurely suppers in the forests' shade!" Earlier scenes are less direct in their scene painting, but they had already indicated briefly the square with Octave in carnival costume, the inn terrace where he sits complaining of the din of the church bells ringing for vespers, the garden with its hired thugs lying in wait. Even more effective, there is the long image tossed like a ball between Octave and Marianne in the first scene of Act II, the image which compares a woman to wine and ends with Octave describing the golden grape clusters by the roadside, the sunshine caressing their curving shapes, thronged by bees; and the thirsty traveler resting beneath the green branches of the vine. None of this, except Octave's speech in the last scene, has the precision with which the city of Florence is portrayed in *Lorenzaccio,* but nevertheless it supplies the play with a picturesque and poetic, if stylized, interpretation of a Mediterranean background.

If a setting can in fact be described as "poetic" in the sense of having the ethereal beauty of reality transfigured by a poet's eyes, then this is one quality that can be found in all but the least successful of Musset's plays. Perhaps the fusion of reality and idealizing appreciation can be seen most clearly when the scene, while still belonging to a magical *où l'on voudra* (wherever you will), seems to have been inspired by French landscape, and probably by the Ile-de-France. *On ne badine pas avec l'amour* brings to our eyes chestnut trees, a lake, a path winding to a farm, a cottage where Rosette is glimpsed at a casement window, a fountain with its surrounding flowers—all the elements of an idyllic countryside. Perdican's sincere emotion when he returns to this *patria chica* makes it all the more difficult to believe with some critics that nature meant comparatively little to Musset.

Shakespeare, too, often took real settings and transformed them into magical places with his dialogue and, whether by chance or because of Musset's admiration for his theater, the background of the *Comédies et Proverbes* often has a Shakespearean look, as for instance in Act III, scene iii of *Il ne faut jurer de rien.* Here Valentin and Van Buck enter a wood; the moon has risen and the earlier storm has died down; the soft breeze stirs the pearls of rain left on the leaves. Lights are seen flickering among the trees, and at last the two lovers, like those of the Forest of Arden, meet in the enchanting woodland setting by moonlight. "See how pure the night is! how the breeze ruffles the jealous tulle around your shoulders! Listen; it is the voice of night, the song of the bird that invites man to joy. Behind this high rock, no eye can see us. All creation is asleep, except those beings who are in love."

In fact, this theater which presents its settings so discreetly, leaves so many charming stage pictures in the mind—the medieval countryside and the castle at dusk in *La Quenouille de Barberine;* the garden in *Le Chandelier* with its plum trees and the honeysuckle trellis—that it is difficult to tear oneself away from lingering over each one in turn. There are memorable interiors too, like Fantasio's depiction of court scenes which have the vividness of Velazquez canvases (Act II, scene ii); or the salon in *Il ne faut jurer de rien* where the baroness works at her tapestry while her daughter learns the fashionable waltz from her dancing master. But Musset's masterpiece of local color is *Lorenzaccio* where the city of Florence is a protagonist almost as important in the play as Lorenzo and the Duke.

Act I opens on a scene which is attractive but not unusual in Romantic plays. There are mysterious comings and goings in a moonlit garden by a summer house, whose lamplight can be seen glimmering through the fig-tree leaves; Maffio sees his sister, bejeweled and with a dark lantern in her hand, crossing the garden. At daybreak, scene ii plunges us into a setting brilliant with color and teeming with the bustle of Florentine streets the morning after a palatial ball. Apprentices and shopkeepers describe vividly the sounds and sights of the past night as masked revelers leave—"Pink, green, blue, my eyes are dazzled; my head is spinning"—while at the same time they introduce central characters and reveal the depths of corruption and tyranny into which Florence had sunk, and the apathy and materialism that merchants of the period shared with those of Musset's age. As a spendidly managed crowd scene, again reminiscent of Shakespeare, this scene is striking for its naturalness and animation, and the component details are accurately filled in. The vague, atmospheric color of *Les Caprices de Marianne* has been replaced by a brilliant, thoroughly documented reconstruction of customs, and yet the spectacle is merely a servant to dramatic purpose and social satire.

Glimpses of the city and its surrounding countryside continue to flash past the reader's eye; sometimes lyrically peaceful as when the Marquise de Cibo dreams of her husband's estate (Act I, scene iii and Act III, scene vi) where love and the landscape seem to be one and the same growth, as they do to Perdican in *On ne badine pas avec l'amour;* sometimes with the kaleidoscopic color and movement of the fair at Montolivet. There are panoramic shots of Florence, as when Catherine describes from outside the walls the sights and sounds of the city at sunset; when Philippe Strozzi, looking from his window, broods over the violence and bloodshed of Florentine streets at night; and when the Marquise, again looking over the city from her window, reflects how many of its houses have been violated by Alexander in his womanizing, and speaks as to a person, beautiful but disgraced. "And why do you have any truck with all this, you, Florence?" At other times the camera moves in to show us a church interior which Musset brings alive for all our senses; a courtyard suddenly filling with page boys and horses as the Duke arrives; Catherine seen at a window arranging flowers; the Arno banks with their line of palaces and terraces at sunset as Lorenzo tries to warn the citizens that he is about to murder their tyrant; the square at night, with a light showing from the church portico and workmen hewing stone as Lorenzo capers in near-delirium before he puts his plan into action.

This visual local color provides only some of the threads which make up the tapestry. Musset's re-creation of the moral and political situation of Florence, a re-creation accurate enough to stand the critics' appraisal, needs a book to itself. Subtly woven into the fabric of the play, there is a complex picture of the elements that make up this society, divided both by status and by political opinion. We are shown the aristocrats, some bestial in their corruption, others idealists full of liberal hopes; beneath them the bourgeoisie, those merchants who fawn on the highborn oppressors whose extravagances, if the bills are finally paid, fill the shop coffers, and others who mutter abuse at the political regime; the apprentices and soldiers in the street; the exiles beyond the city gates. The spectator or the reader is never aware that he is being taught political history, for the picture is built up unobtrusively as the plot progresses. Sometimes Musset uses comments from the characters, as when the goldsmith depicts in an extended image the structure and corruption of Florentine society (Act I, scene ii). At other times, as in the first scene where the Duke entices from her home a young recruit-courtesan whom Lorenzo has spied out for him, incidents serve as object lessons.

The sinister, corrupt, and violent atmosphere closes in upon the reader, but Musset gives a balanced picture through such figures as Tebaldeo, the young painter, with his love and reverence for Florence as mother of the arts. This struggle between the forces of corruption and good is a vital part of the plot, for on the citizens' reaction to the tyrant's murder depends the validity, from the practical point of view, of Lorenzo's action. As he foresaw, the force of evil backed by mass apathy wins the day, and in the final scene the wheel has come full circle as German soldiers, standing by while the new rule of tyranny is established, manhandle the crowds as they did in the first act. To my mind, such settings fulfil all that the *Préface de Cromwell* requires while avoiding the overlushness or garishness to which Romanticism was prone, and it is strange that Musset fails to follow another precept of the *Préface,* as we shall now see.

III *Dialogue*

Victor Hugo, orchestrating his own plays with superb verse, recommended all Romantic dramatists to versify their dialogue, but when Musset attempted to do so the result was sometimes surprisingly mediocre, as in *Louison.* Yet on another score—the mingling of comedy and tragedy—the dialogue of the *Comédies et Proverbes* again puts the theory of the *Préface* into excellent practice. We have already seen Musset's poetry flash with humor, but it is in the theater that his wit, fantasy, and sometimes sheer buffoonery flare out in their full force. For all the common image of him as melancholy and lovesick, he belongs to the lineage of great comic writers, yet has a comic style that is distinctively his own.

Occasionally his verbal humor follows one of the straightforward traditional patterns still used by comedians, as in the cross-talk of *Il ne faut jurer de rien* (Act I, scene ii), when the Baroness, carrying on two conversations and one monologue at the same time, seems to accuse the Abbé of sitting on Miss Clary when it is her lost skein of tapestry wool that she has in mind. More often, however, comic passages can be divided into two categories. The first introduces us to Musset's caricatures—the grotesques—either singly or in pairs. The hilarious word battles in which they are involved are both stylized and true to life, and one pattern used in *Les Caprices de Marianne* and *Fantasio* consists of an exchange of comic insults or sarcastic descriptions rising to a climax of vituperation. When Claudio and Octave cross verbal swords in *Les Caprices,* this crescendo is built up by another favorite device in the *Comédies et Proverbes,* the near-echo effect in which the pattern of the first speaker's line of dialogue is repeated by the second speaker until the reader feels as though he were listening to a verse-speaking recital:

CLAUDIO: Incidentally, seigneur Octave, it seems to me that my door-knocker has every appearance of having burnt your fingers.

OCTAVE: How is that, most knowledgeable judge?

CLAUDIO: When you tried to rap at the door, most subtle cousin.

OCTAVE: You should add that I did so with the greatest respect for your door-knocker, judge; but you can repaint it without my having any fear of finding paint on my fingers.

CLAUDIO: How is that, most waggish cousin?

OCTAVE: Because I shall never lay a finger on it, most caustic judge.

CLAUDIO: But you must have done so already, since my wife has ordered her servants to slam the door in your face as soon as you appear.

OCTAVE: Your spectacles are short-sighted, most gracious judge: your compliment is directed to the wrong address.

CLAUDIO: My spectacles are excellent, most argumentative cousin: have you not made a declaration of love to my wife?

OCTAVE: On whose behalf, perceptive magistrate?

CLAUDIO: On behalf of your friend Coelio, cousin; unfortunately I heard everything.

OCTAVE: With which ear, incorruptible senator?

CLAUDIO: With my wife's: she told me everything, dear wastrel.

OCTAVE: Absolutely everything, revered judge? Nothing remained in that charming ear?

CLAUDIO: Nothing but her reply, which it is my duty to convey to you, charming propper-up of bars.

OCTAVE: It is no duty of mine to listen to it, dear minutes-of-the-last-meeting.

CLAUDIO: My door will give you the message, then, genial roulette croupier, if you take it into your head to consult it.

OCTAVE: That is the last thing I should think of doing, dear death-sentence; I can live happily without that.

CLAUDIO: May you do so in peace, dear dice-box. I wish you every prosperity.

OCTAVE: Rest assured, dear prison bolt! I sleep as peacefully as though I were in your court-room. (Act II, scene i)

There is descriptive humor too, as in the lines preceding the passage quoted above, where Octave depicts Claudio's legs as "two charming parentheses"; and sometimes there is purely verbal humor, as when the prince in *Fantasio* orders his aide-de-camp to "write in a low voice." Perhaps one of the most memorable comic speeches is a monologue in which Bridaine, one of the trio of grotesques in *On ne badine pas avec l'amour,* delivers himself of a masterpiece of mock-heroic eloquence, appropriating the language of the Classical tragedy to apply it to his lost comforts: "Farewell, venerable armchair where I have reclined so often, replete with succulent dainties! ... Farewell, magnificent table, noble dining-room, never again shall I pronounce the blessing!" (Act II, scene ii).

At other times it is the conscious wit of Musset's heroes rather than the unconscious humor of the buffoons which adds sparkle to the dialogue. Here, perhaps, it is possible to trace a change, a decrescendo, between the earlier and later plays. It is true that *Il faut qu'une porte soit ouverte ou fermée,* first published in 1845, glitters with sophisticated humor somewhat in the fashion of Oscar Wilde's *The Importance of Being Earnest;* and the Count, for instance, paints an unforgettable picture of trying to hold a conversation among the din of trombones and tinkling glasses in a crowded ballroom, where other guests tread on one's feet or jog one's elbow and a waiter misfires with the ice cream he is carrying, dropping it into one's pocket. Yet it is Octave in *Les Caprices de Marianne* of 1833 and above all Fantasio, in the play which appeared in 1834, that show Musset's exuberant wit cascading in its full force. Lorenzaccio, Fantasio's elder brother in this theater, has the same sharp intelligence and the same power to spin word-pictures, but the sourness of his experience has turned his laughter to a wry grimace.

Fantasio, on the other hand, incarnates all the gaiety of the Musset who in the comparatively carefree days of the Quai Malaquais was quite capable of joining with his friends in the sort of prank that set the Prince of Mantua's wig dangling in the air at the end of a fishing line. The whole of Fantasio's conversation with Spark in Act I, scene ii is a virtuoso's display of verbal humor, decorating the underlying seriousness of the problem discussed—the sickness of the hero's generation— sometimes with a pun, sometimes with a piece of comic fantasy as when he imagines himself enamored of a ballet dancer and finally dying in her arms of a surfeit of strawberries; sometimes by the linking of disparate objects—"Oh! I wish I could feel a grand passion for lobster with mustard sauce, for a *grisette,* for a class of minerals." When he puts on the costume of a court fool he has no need to do anything but let his wit flow on as before in puns, comic personifications, and descriptions such as that of the elaborate protocol involved in a new jester being accepted by the palace staff.

Witty dialogue, so fanciful and ethereal that it disintegrates like spun sugar at the translator's touch, is one of the distinguishing marks of this theater, but its apparent fragility masks the strength that comes from being accurately copied from real life. Both *André del Sarto* and *Lorenzaccio* show how Musset can reproduce convincingly the speech of a man close to delirium; at the other end of the emotional scale, we hear him in *Un Caprice* reflecting in the subtly changing undertones of domestic conversation the nuances of the relationship between husband and wife.

It is the unusual but highly effective marriage of this naturalness with poetry in Musset's dialogue which critics have recognized as one of the qualities which set him above most other Romantic dramatists. His lines do not set out to reach the sheer magnificence, the towering scale of, for instance, Don Carlos' monologue in front of Charlemagne's tomb in Hugo's *Hernani,* and his love scenes have not the full-blown, heady richness of some of the dialogues between Hernani and Doña Sol, but their poetic quality is no less great. As far as variety of mood and theme is concerned, Musset, far from restricting himself to the solo violin of plaintive love, has a whole orchestra of effects at his command. When Philippe Strozzi speaks of his murdered daughter in Act IV, scene v of *Lorenzaccio,* the lyricism of grieving fatherly affection is as touching as in many of Hugo's famous treatments of this theme and, in absolute contrast, there are the superb cameos of the arrival of Blazius and Dame Pluche at the beginning of *On ne badine pas avec l'amour,* superb because of the skill with which Musset handles language to paint with a few strokes both figures and landscape with a humor, a picturesqueness, and a poetry that remind one of illustrations on medieval manuscripts.

These flashes of true poetry in prose, occurring rarely but leaving an ineradicable mark in the memories of readers susceptible to such things, often take the shape of original images, some developed at length and passed to and fro between a pair of characters in conversation. Fantasio and Elsbeth with their debated comparison of the metamorphosis of flowers and marriages of convenience bring into Act II, scene i the shapes, colors, and by implication the scents of the palace flower garden. Indeed, *Fantasio* as a whole is like a firework display of images, visually arresting and always significant for the point they make about a character or an idea. In Act II, scene v, for instance, there is the exquisite yet socially satirical depiction of a girl of good family demonstrating her carefully inculcated airs and graces to a suitor. Musset compares her to a toy singing bird, and her prepared flow of words to a magical fountain around which all the social conventions dance on tiptoe-like nymphs.

Here again Musset is a past master at an art the Romantics rated highly—the writing of poetic, picturesque dialogue and the use of images to explore personality—but once again he never allows his ability to run riot and escape from subordination to his main dramatic purpose. Many plays have scarcely any metaphors or similes except those which have become built into everyday speech, and where an explosion of imagery occurs it either suits the role of the speaker (Fantasio, after all, is a court fool for most of the play), or else it is generated by a scene of great emotional intensity, as in the interview in which Lorenzaccio reveals the secrets of his life to Philippe Strozzi in Act III, scene iii. In passages like these, the comparison sometimes made with Shakespearean plays does not seem an impertinence, and yet both the style and the content are unmistakably stamped with Musset's individual characteristics and those of his period and nationality.

IV *Plots*

It is above all the way in which his plots are constructed that shows how closely Musset's dramatic technique could follow the French Classical pattern at times. Occasionally a scene such as that in *Le Chandelier* where a justifiably angry husband is cleverly transformed by his wife's guile into a penitent one, or the comic dialogue at the opening of *Il ne faut jurer de rien* where a young man and his enraged provider debate money and extravagance, or the traditional scheming of a loyal manservant and maid in *On ne saurait penser à tout* have a definitely Molièresque ring about them, but in most of the successful plays it is the more fundamental matter of the tautness of the action and the careful preparation of the denouement which bring to mind the best of French seventeenth-century drama. Musset's plots may seem to move like fantasias, following the characters' or the author's whim, and it is true that it is sometimes Shakespeare's example he follows in stringing together a swift succession of short scenes, but beneath the apparent capriciousness of kaleidoscopic scenes a closer look reveals that the action progresses as inexorably and excludes the irrelevant as ruthlessly as do Racine's plots, whose movement Lytton Strachey compared to escalators.

André del Sarto seems to me one of the most striking examples of Musset's skill at organizing the movement of a plot. The opening lines of dialogue reproduce a cliché of the Romantic stage—night in Italy, a man enveloped in a cloak climbs from his mistress's window, strikes with his dagger at the servant who tries to intercept him, and escapes into the darkness of the garden. There hackneyed Romanticism ends, and the play develops on far more individual lines than the opening would lead an audience to expect. Immediately a touch of comedy lightens the atmosphere as Damien, André's friend, tries to persuade the wounded and irate servant that he is drunk and incapable of seeing clearly. By the time Grémio, still swearing to the reality of what he saw, leaves the stage, the audience's interest has been aroused not only by the mysterious intruder but by Damien's reasons for wishing to silence the witness.

The characters of the comic but trusty porter and of Damien as the wise friend are already sketched in, and the next section of scene i reveals the identity of the cloaked figure and searchingly, though briefly, explores the situation in which he finds himself. Our sympathy is aroused at the same time for the lover and for the deceived husband, so that the play's point of departure is more complex and more true to life than the usual Romantic version of the eternal triangle. By the end of the short first scene several of the main characters have been established rapidly but decisively, and the spectator has been put in the picture about André's domestic situation. Insight into the other crucial side of his life, his professional affairs, follows in the second scene, and the action is sent speeding on its way as André tells Grémio of the plan whose consequences form the climax of the next scene.

This third and last scene of Act I compresses into a short space a surprising amount of information, action, and variety, both in pace and in the imagined stage picture. As happened with Cordiani and André, the lover and the tricked husband, so Lucrèce's conflict-torn character is briefly explored, so that our sympathy for her is roused far more than it is for the usual pasteboard figure of the Romantic heroine who finds herself in this situation. The action continues its taut way as the news of the French envoys' expected arrival is followed by Grémio's dying cry and Cordiani's arrival in the room. The stage, which near the beginning of the scene had shown only Lucrèce at prayer, fills and then empties, leaving André gazing at the blood-covered hand which tells him that his friend Cordiani is both Grémio's murderer and Lucrèce's lover.

Act II delves into André's mind and emotions and at the same time brings the violent, even melodramatic action of the duel fought by night while the thunder rolls, leaving him soliloquizing on the horror he feels in the deserted house, empty of his wife's presence. Then the third act moves along its streamlined way to the denouement, but nevertheless takes time to throw an indication to the reader of what the ending will be. In scene i, André, in his near-delirious ramblings, tells Lionel that he has bought poison, so that we are prepared, almost as in a Classical tragedy, for what is to happen. In the following scene the French envoy puts the greatness of André as a painter into perspective, making us aware of the double tragedy of his suicide as the destruction of a first-rate artist as well as the death of a man in despair. The very last episodes—the suicide, and the bringing of the news to Lucrèce and Cordiani as they are fleeing from the city—are pared down to the utmost brevity. Although André dies on the stage, there is no hint of melodrama, and we hear no self-pitying outpourings. It is as though André and Lucrèce are emotionally in touch now as they had not been earlier in the play, for André describes her flight as though he is gifted with second sight, and she is full of foreboding as she rides away. In short, this Romantic plot is unfolded with the controlled terseness, rapidity, and restraint of the best Classical plays.

This skill in dramatic construction—a skill that is highly disciplined and professional—runs quite contrary to the usual idea of Musset as a gifted but negligent dilettante of letters, and it is hard to think of an occasion on which it fails him. In *Les Caprices de Marianne* in particular, despite the title, the denouement is prepared from the very first scene where Coelio, at the moment of asking Octave to intercede for him with Marianne, is filled with foreboding that his friend will deceive him. The story of his mother's courtship, told in scene ii, repeats the somber betrayal theme, and to heighten the final tragedy it is Octave in Act II, scene i who insists that the siege of Marianne should continue when Coelio is ready to abandon it. There is irony in his comparison of himself to a gambler playing on another's behalf and ready to ruin his friend rather than admit defeat. In fact, in the best Classical tradition he contributes himself to the disaster which, with the physical death of his friend, brings spiritual death to the better part of himself. The death of the hero by an assassin's knife as he enters his would-be mistress's garden may seem a Romantic coup de théâtre, but even this resembles the Classical pattern. Not only has Coelio had premonitions of this death throughout the play, but at the last he walks into the ambush in an act of virtual suicide. He chooses death, he does not have it thrust upon him by an accident of fate.

[101]

Readers sometimes complain that *On ne badine pas avec l'amour* is spoiled for them by the sudden violence of the last scene, when Rosette, hearing Camille and Perdican at last confessing their love for each other, falls dead behind the altar. It is true that, handled differently, this conclusion might have been both melodramatic and improbable, but Musset presents with a Racinian starkness an event for which both the reader and the two main characters should have been prepared by the earlier scene in which Rosette, hidden by Camille behind a curtain, faints when she hears the lovers' conversation (III. vi). Even earlier, in Act I, scene iv, the Chorus tries to prevent Perdican from first approaching Rosette, as though it foresaw inevitably tragic results. In fact, the final dramatic shock to the reader's nerves is no less well prepared than the ending of *Phèdre*.

In his introduction of a chorus Musset outdoes the French Classicists themselves in borrowing from Greek tragedy, and he squeezes every ounce of dramatic usefulness from a device which might well have been mere artificial ornament. Not only does the group of peasants sometimes act as the omniscient bystander, a figure whom twentieth-century dramatists often put on the stage and scenario writers on the movie screen (in the guise of a traveling musician, for instance, in Cocteau's *Orphée)*, but in the first scene it serves to introduce the characters, to set the scene, and, in the dialogue with Pluche and Blazius as they arrive, to give the audience all the knowledge it needs of previous events. In a few lines, both vivid and amusing, the Chorus supplies all that is needed for an opening scene. Musset makes no attempt to disguise the artificiality of his device, but rather makes this very artificiality an asset by emphasizing it and making the whole scene charmingly stylized—charming, that is, for those who are not allergic to this brand of fantasy. There is the symmetrical repetition and contrast typical of fairy tales as first the fat priest and then the bony governess are described by the Chorus, give a characteristic greeting to them, and ask for a drink—Blazius for wine and, symbolically, Dame Pluche for water and vinegar.

Much has been written about the action of *Lorenzaccio,* a mazelike plot where interconnecting stories are traced and combined with the utmost skill and clarity, each adding its essential contribution to the characterization of the two main forces in the play—Lorenzaccio himself and the city of Florence. At first the reader is presented with the enigma of Lorenzaccio as his family and fellow citizens see him; then in the central and crucial third scene of Act III he himself explains the mystery of his character and actions, clearly indicating the course of events which must logically follow from the interaction of his plan and his personality with the nature of Florentine society. From this point, which seems to me the climax of the play rather than the murder scene, the foretold action moves swiftly and inevitably to the close of a plot which is a feat of complicated dramatic engineering. At the end, the wheel has come full circle with the enthroning of the new despot. Lorenzo has been murdered and, as he prophesied, the heroic act which gave meaning to his life has been utterly useless to his fellow men.

From the technical point of view, the play is perhaps most famous for its Shakespearean stringing together of short scenes, almost as though a Corpus Christi procession, presenting tableau after tableau, were moving in front of the reader. This is one of the uses to which Musset puts his freedom from the demands and limitations of the contemporary stage, but *Lorenzaccio* also shows that he knows how to handle a dramatic incident on the grand traditional lines, in the conspirators' banquet scene where Louise is poisoned (Act III, scene vii). Above all, the action deserves admiration for its ruthless concentration on essential elements. The first of the deleted scenes reproduced in Van Tieghem's edition contributes less directly to the denouement and has less cohesion than those which were retained.

It may be true that the events of everyday life resemble the unexpected twists and turns of Romantic plots more often than the logical progression of Classical plays, but from the esthetic point of view there is great satisfaction in watching the cleverly prepared, apparently spontaneous unfolding of Musset's plots. When Hugo is in the process of linking together his splendid or moving dramatic spectacles, one sometimes feels as though one can hear the clanking and grinding of clumsy machinery, but Musset constructs a play with an ease which hides his skill. At a time when plots tended to be sensational, overintricate, and more important than the characters, his plots show concision, restraint, clarity, and inevitability, the hallmarks of the great seventeenth-century dramatists. Perhaps it is an oversimplification to label these qualities in his theater as "Classical," for they help to spell dramatic success in any period.

V *Themes and Ideas*

Probably most people would grant that Musset was a skilled dramatic technician, but would criticize him as a lightweight as far as the content of ideas in his plays is concerned. In this age when the existence of a portentous "message" is sometimes allowed to excuse the lack of almost anything else in the theater, any dramatist who weaves his thought into the fabric of his work as unobtrusively as Musset does is almost certain to meet sneers. It is probable that the solemnity of later "thesis" plays would have amused him as much as the extravagances and absurdities of some plays of his own time, but nevertheless he himself had something to say about the problems of life, less the spectacular problems which beset man as a political being than those more intimate and universal ones which affect a man's relationship with himself and with those closest to him, and also his attitude to life itself. Even here, it will be argued, his range was restricted largely to the interaction of young people on each other, but it must be remembered that most of his plays were written while he was under thirty years of age, when his experience of life and his concerns were necessarily those of a young man. This does not prevent him from speaking on the themes which he treats with a perceptiveness and a wisdom which have as much to say to following generations as to his own.

The main theme of most of the *Comédies et Proverbes* is love, though it is often intertwined with another favorite subject—the corrosion of character by cynicism, debauchery, and boredom—which flowers magnificently in *Lorenzaccio* to the exclusion of love. Musset does not specialize as Marivaux does in studying one particular phase in the relationship of a man and a woman, but he has all Marivaux's subtlety in reflecting in dialogue the almost imperceptible nuances of changing attitude as one character becomes attracted to another. Marianne and Camille, proudly entrenched in their convent-taught certainties, are both brought to a new self-awareness and challenged with a new outlook on life which finally breaks down their hostility toward Octave and Perdican, respectively. In *Fantasio,* although this is not the central theme, Musset traces by even more delicate gradations the Princess's cold reception of the impertinent new jester turning into such grateful sympathy that one is left wondering how much she regrets that he is not the Prince of Mantua in disguise, as her governess had supposed. This awakening of emotion probably appears more often in the plays than the other stages in love's progress, but Musset can show too the full blaze of triumphant passion in Cordiani *(André del Sarto),* or the despairing secret longing that almost destroys Carmosine after she has fallen in love with her king.

Strangely enough it is Octave, the cynic, who in *Les Caprices de Marianne* shows to what an extent Musset's conception of love could sometimes typify what is generally expected of Romanticism. He describes it as the most cruel of maladies, for it is without hope; the most terrible, for it is a malady which cherishes itself, and rejects the healing cup even from the hand of a friend; a malady which makes lips grow pallid with poisons sweeter than ambrosia, and which makes the hardest heart melt into raining tears, like Cleopatra's pearl; a malady which all herbs, all human skills are powerless to ease, and which feeds on the passing breeze, the scent of a faded rose, the chorus of a song, and which sucks the never failing nourishment of its sufferings from all that surrounds it, as a bee does its honey from every bush in the garden. (Act I, scene i)

Far better known and even more extreme is Perdican's credo in the final scene of Act II in *On ne badine pas avec l'amour,* a credo which, as far as its last statement is concerned, is like a banner waving over the whole of Musset's work:

All men are liars, fickle, false, tittle-tattling, hypocritical, vainglorious and cowardly, despicable and sensual; all women are faithless, scheming, vain, inquisitive, and depraved; the world is no more than a bottomless sewer where the most misshapen seals crawl and writhe over mounds of filth; but there is one sacred and sublime thing in the world, it is the union of two of these misformed and hideous creatures. A man is often deceived in love, often hurt, and often wretched; but he loves, and when he is at the grave's edge he looks back and says: "I have often suffered, sometimes I have been mistaken, but I have loved. It is I myself who have lived, and not a dummy created by my pride and my boredom."

Some eleven years after the publication of this play, toward the end of Musset's productive years as a dramatist, his views on this subject were unchanged. The Count in *Il faut qu'une porte soit ouverte ou fermée* is an older Perdican, incensed by the Marchioness's sneers at love, which for him is eternal and paramount—"Love is dead, long live Love!"

Other readers will no doubt find the acme of Romantic love in *Carmosine* whose whole theme is the heroine's narrow escape from a death which would have been caused solely by her closely guarded secret, her consuming love for the man whom she has scarcely seen. The languishing heroine is a stock joke for those who find Romantic works amusing, but Musset makes it clear that he is not so much relating a conventional story as putting on stage a situation which he firmly believes possible. In Act III, scene viii the Queen declares that those who deny that such a secret, hopeless love can cause death, in a woman at least, do not know what they are talking about. A man can find a cure in his career, but the needle or the spinning wheel which occupy a girl's fingers cannot fully occupy her thoughts, and her grief grows all the deeper because the world's mockery forces her to wall it up within herself. To some extent, changing society and the partial emancipation of women have made this study a period piece, but its observation of emotions is still true.

Full-blown Romanticism can be found too in the religious imagery which Cordiani uses to describe the bliss of love *(André del Sarto,* Act I, scene i). "Oh! my God! joy is a sublime altar. May my soul's joy rise to Thee like sweet incense!" In that age, love for a woman was indeed almost turned into a religion, as it had been in the days of courtly love. The intoxication of shared love is for Cordiani what Musset sought for himself—an all-powerful and unifying force which invades his personality and forms the magnetic center for all his earlier vague desires and hopes. There is a certain modernity about this Romanticism, for it raises a question which could probably not have been asked in Classical French literature. A seventeenth-century character who had fallen into adulterous love would not have been in doubt about the moral issues involved but, like many a twentieth-century character, Cordiani cannot accept that this love which he believes the greatest good in his life can be sinful.

Am I guilty today? Then why am I happy? And, besides, what can you say to me that I have not already said a hundred times over to myself? Am I a heartless libertine? Am I an atheist? Have I ever spoken slightingly of all those sacred words which, since the world began, have hovered in vain on men's lips? I have leveled at myself every possible reproach, and still I am happy. Remorse, terrible vengeance, sad and silent grief, all these dread specters have presented themselves at my door; none could hold their ground against the love of Lucretia.

At a period, then, when the emotions in general, freed from the shackles of the cult of reason, were put on a pedestal and passionate love, on the highest pedestal of all, when some men tried to find in their relationship with a woman a substitute for a relationship with God, and when the modern tendency emerged to believe that passion was justified in overriding any duty, Musset was in the very vanguard of Romanticism. Yet nowadays the term "Romantic love" often has a pejorative ring about it; it implies that the feelings described are probably highly unreal and that they are exaggerated even to the point of being ridiculous. This is true of second-rate Romantic writers, and some readers may even think it applies to the first rank too; but for

Musset, love was too vital a matter to be treated other than with the greatest realism of which he was capable. I believe that he succeeds in analyzing universal emotion so accurately that, beneath the nineteenth-century trimmings, men of any generation can recognize their own reactions in his characters. Lovers may meet more by neon street lights than by moonlight nowadays, but they still sometimes act out the roles of Camille, Perdican, and Rosette, or those of Coelio, Octave, and Marianne, with twentieth-century modifications, and countless modern "lyrics" give fresh expression to Fortunio's description of love from a distance: "I lived in the shadow of your life. You spent the morning at your doorway, at night I returned to weep there. When a few words from your lips reached my ears, I repeated them the whole day long. You grew flowers, my room was full of them. You sang at your piano in the evening, I knew your songs by heart. Everything that you loved, I loved; I was intoxicated with everything that came from your lips or your heart" *(Le Chandelier,* Act II, scene iv).

Two other themes pervade Musset's theater—the nature of life and the role of women in society—but the second of these is treated so unobtrusively, although tellingly, that at a first reading it is easy to overlook how insistently Musset returns to his ideas on the subject. We have already seen in the short stories how concerned he was about the position women occupied in the community, but in the theater he makes his case with even greater force. As early as 1830, *La Nuit vénitienne* opens with the theme of the girl "sold" in marriage regardless of her inclinations. Razetta describes with loathing Laurette's arranged marriage: "And you, your heart, your head, your life, haggled over by go-betweens, all has been sold to the highest bidder" (Act I, scene i).

Les Caprices de Marianne presents us with the after effects of such a marriage. Marianne is a far more complex character than one would expect from the length of the play or the nature of its plot. On first acquaintance she seems odious to some readers, who see her as a proud and quick-tempered prude who is largely responsible for Coelio's death, as the title suggests, but a closer study shows that she is at the mercy of her circumstances as much as, if not more than, Coelio. Passing references to her history tell us that she was convent-reared and was then married by a seemingly dominant mother to her monumentally pompous and stupid husband. When Octave taunts her with her indifference to Coelio's advances, she replies bitterly, commenting on the situation of women like herself with an intelligence and a dignity which discountenance even the blasé Octave, and which even Musset to his astonishment found it difficult to counter in Octave's answering speech. Coelio has fallen in love with her, she says, whereupon his friends have decreed that she shall at all costs be his mistress. If she yields meekly to their orders that she shall love Coelio within the week, she will be the talk of the town. If she refuses, she is open to abuse as a frigid monster. "What a ridiculous thing is integrity and sworn faithfulness, a girl's education, the pride of a heart which imagines that it is not without value and that before the pollen of its carefully nurtured flower is cast on the wind its calyx must be bedewed with falling tears, brought to full bloom by a few rays of sunshine, opened by delicate finger tips. Is all this anything more than a dream, a soap-bubble that must shatter at a dandy's first sigh?" (Act II, scene i). Most men, she adds before she sweeps out, look on a woman as one night of pleasure; only to the naïve does she represent the potential happiness of a lifetime.

Haughty, acid-tongued, and impulsive she may be, but after her interchanges with Octave she appears no longer as a doll-like prude but as a tormented and hard-pressed young woman trying to live up to the code of right and duty which all her upbringing has instilled in her. It is society's fault, not hers, that this code has bound her to a marriage in which there is little chance of mutual esteem, let alone affection, developing. The marriage to which she has been obliged to vow lifelong fidelity cannot even begin to satisfy her emotional needs, and so when at last her heart is touched, disaster of some sort is almost inevitable.

Fantasio, beneath its fairy-tale surface, adds its witty, brightly imaged yet pungent attacks on the theme of the girl whose dreams have been nourished on novelettes and romances, yet who is reared to prostitute her whole self in a marriage of materialistic convenience. Indeed it is said to be an incident of this type, the wedding of Princess Louise of France to King Leopold I of Belgium, that moved Musset to write the play. Perdican takes up even more savagely in *On ne badine pas avec l'amour* the denouncement of convent education, and Lorenzaccio comments on the disastrous way in which the bourgeoisie brings up its daughters with no solid education, but merely a veneer of elegance (Act I, scene i), and on the miseries of those who have been seduced (Act IV, scene v).

On a less serious plane, but still with the same basic idea of men's general underestimation of women, *Un Caprice* brings to book Chavigny who is guilty of asking: "Can women be permitted to live on an equal footing with us? The absurdity of the idea hits one in the face" (scene viii); and in *Il faut qu'une porte soit ouverte ou fermée* the

Marchioness laments that men cannot treat women as intelligent beings instead of boring them at social functions with the sole topic of their prettiness. These portraits and comments make it easy to guess what sort of changes Musset would like to have seen in the upbringing of girls and the position of women in society, and in *Il ne faut jurer de rien* Valentin ends a spirited attack on the education of fashionable young women with at least an indication of the positive side of Musset's ideas: "I would rather that a girl were a wild flower in a wood, and not a plant under glass." Musset may have written no treatise on feminine education or marriage reform, but clearly he saw women not only as "these charming, indefinable beings" who make their ethereal way through his plays but also as very real human beings, often oppressed by society. Nor, on the other hand, does he forget to comment on the dandyism and debauchery of the young men of the day.

Curiosity makes one wish that he had been as explicit about his ideal education as Montaigne was and, when one finds recurring the theme of the strangeness of life, again it is tantalizing to have Musset's ideas merely reflected in his characters, instead of set out in full. Coelio in *Les Caprices de Marianne* describes exquisitely the enchanting mirage toward which a man in love drifts, and goes on to declare that reality is no more than a shadow. "Every man walks through life wrapped in a transparent net which covers him from head to foot: he thinks he sees woods and rivers, divine faces, and universal nature takes on beneath his gaze the countless tints of the magic fabric" (Act I, scene i). This feeling that the reality of life is as baffling as a gallery of distorting mirrors fits in well with Coelio's melancholy, introspective temperament, but when Octave, the cynical *bon vivant*, depicts his own life in a long image in the same scene, this too has the quality of a phantasmagoria—a nightmarish one in this instance—and later it is he who puts into words another recurring idea, the idea that life itself is basically capricious. "The man who works out the odds, who enrolls reason on his side is mad, raving mad. Divine justice holds scales in its hands. The scales are perfectly true, but all the weights are hollow. In one there is a gold coin, in the other a lover's sigh, in one a migraine, in the other the weather that particular day, and all human actions find their level according to these capricious weights" (Act II, scene iv).

For Fantasio too "everything here on earth is a pun, and it is as difficult to understand the expression on the face of a four-year-old child as the rigmarole of three modern plays" (Act II, scene i). There is nothing new in the idea of how difficult it is to fix the boundary between reality and illusion, or the apparent haphazardness of life, nor about Fantasio's reminder how every human being is totally isolated from every other amid the banalities of everyday conversation (Act I, scene ii). Yet all these are themes which were perhaps less to the fore in the minds of the more authoritarian seventeenth century with its greater religious orthodoxy, or the eighteenth century with its belief in reason, but which have come more and more into prominence in the twentieth century. Musset feels and expresses such problems as the difficulty of any real communication between human beings with an intensity which sometimes gives a strangely modern ring to his dialogue. "Alas! everything that men say to each other follows the same pattern; the ideas that they exchange are almost always the same in all their conversation; but, within all these solitary machines, what nooks and crannies, what secret compartments there are! Each of us carries a whole world within himself! an undiscovered world that is born and dies in silence! What wastes of loneliness are all these human bodies!" *(Fantasio,* Act I, scene ii). I am not suggesting that Musset was a profound philosopher, but his theater seems to me to show, as Hugo's rarely does, a keen awareness of some of the problems about life itself which have particularly preoccupied men in the last two centuries. Again one must remember the youthfulness of this man whose imagery could crystallize human loneliness and bewilderment.

From time to time there is a glimpse of his views on art, on the artist's code of integrity and the conflict between life and art. The discussions in André del Sarto's studio allow Musset to criticize, through comments on the Italy in which the play is set, his own day when artists "work to make a living, and the arts become mere crafts" (Act I, scene i). Similarly André answers his cocky apprentice's demand for something new in art by pointing out the contrast between the novelty for which many seek and the eternal renewal and yet sameness of nature. Perhaps it is Musset speaking to the Romantic school when André declares that the task of the young artist is not to change everything but to take over the torch of tradition with reverence. Certainly it is his contemporaries with their search for beauty in the fantastic and the exotic that he blames in *Le Songe d'Auguste* (first fragment) for overlooking beauty where it is most to be found—all around them in their everyday life, in a blade of grass growing by a path, in the green foliage of the almond trees turned white by the rain. Act II, scene ii in *André del Sarto* shows us the remorse of a man who has been torn between the need to produce works of art as fast as possible in order to heap luxuries on the woman he loved, and the artistic integrity which demanded that no picture should leave his studio one second before it was completed to his satisfaction. *Lorenzaccio* too has its esthetic discussions, on which nations produce great art and on the artist's task in realizing his dreams on canvas (Act II, scene ii).

On a comic level, Musset's opinions of contemporary literature afford us the delightful picture of M. Vertigo giving a reading of his tear-jerking melodrama *(On ne saurait penser à tout,* scene i), and a splendid parody of Hernani, Ruy Blas, or any stereotyped Romantic hero in the Prince of Mantua's address to Elsbeth:

How happy are the noblemen of the world! They can marry you, I cannot; it is quite impossible for me to do so; I am of lowly birth; my only fortune is a name feared by the enemy; a pure, unsullied heart beats beneath this modest uniform; I am a poor soldier riddled with bullets from head to foot; I have not a single ducat; I am alone, exiled from my native land as from my heavenly home, that is to say the paradise of my dreams; I have no woman's heart to press against my heart; I am accursed and silent. *(Fantasio,* Act II, scene ii)

Much as art meant to Musset, it seems to lose the duel with life and its other pleasures as far as he was concerned. Fantasio declares roundly that a glass of wine is better than a sonnet (Act I, scene ii), and surely it is Musset speaking when Perdican tells the chorus of villagers that "learning is a fine thing, my children; these trees and meadows proclaim at the top of their voices the greatest wisdom of all, to forget what one has learned" *(On ne badine pas avec l'amour,* Act I, scene iv).

VI *"Grotesques" and "Grisâtres"*

The *Comédies et Proverbes,* then, are not without ideas, although, as with the society women of Musset's day, these sometimes pass unnoticed beneath superficial lightness and attractiveness. Yet if Musset's claims to greatness as a playwright had to be championed by one single aspect of his works, it would surely be his power to create characters that would serve him best, and among his characters some of the most original are his "grotesques"—the pompous, laughable figures who bumble their way among the seriously portrayed dramatis personae, much as Bottom and his fellow rustics do among the "Immortals" in *A Midsummer Night's Dream.* Their comic procession marches right through the plays, from the Marquis who adds an early sketch of a grotesque to *La Nuit vénitienne,* to the extravagantly methodical Baron in *On ne saurait penser à tout.* Both are obsessed with time, and the Baron is infuriated by the untidy way in which haphazard life upsets his metronome-like calculations. We have already heard Octave declare that life is anything but orderly, and in the portrait of another baron, Perdican's father in *On ne badine pas avec l'amour,* Musset again pokes fun at a man who prearranges life as if it were a mathematical calculation, only to find reality throwing his schemes into chaos.

Even the somberness of *Lorenzaccio* is lightened by two hyper-pedantic tutors and by Lorenzo's Uncle Bindo and his friend Venturi. The humorous effect of the latter pair is heightened because they knock and enter at a moment when Lorenzo's emotion is intense, interrupting it with the pompous snobbishness which was another of Musset's favorite targets. "Sir, I am at the head of a silk-factory," says Venturi, "but it is an insult to call me a merchant" (Act II, scene iv). Rosemberg in *La Quenouille de Barberine* gives a solo performance as a grotesque, but probably the best examples occur in two duets of stupidity and pomposity—Claudio and Tibia in *Les Caprices de Marianne* and the Prince and his valet in *Fantasio*—and in one superb trio of caricatures in *On ne badine pas avec l'amour.*

The first passage of dialogue between Claudio and his valet meanders through a series of irrelevancies and quibbles over detail back to its starting point, the discussion of what action he is to take about his wife's serenaders (Act I, scene iii). Octave prepares us for Claudio's appearance by describing him as a "village pedant" (Act I, scene i), and his stupidity consists of lack of judgment, not witlessness or lack of education. The first scene of Act II shows that he is quick-tongued enough to keep up his side of the verbal duel with Octave, but at the end of Act I he had reached entirely the wrong conclusion about Marianne's behavior through the overtortuousness of his mind, reading guile into her words when they were to be taken at face value. It is this combination of power—he is a judge—with overweening pride, lack of humor, and lack of discrimination which Musset rightly shows to be sinister. Claudio and Tibia as caricatures have the nightmarish quality of a Goya study. In their first dialogue Tibia declares blandly that "the death sentence is a splendid thing to pronounce," and Claudio arranges the assassination of Marianne's supposed lover and the safe disposal of his corpse with dispatch and efficiency.

As with Molière's potentially tragic Alceste in *Le Misanthrope,* it is difficult to know how much the author himself meant to be read into this dark side of his caricature. It is true that *Fantasio's* Prince of Mantua has a sinister potential too in the threatening shadow he casts over Elsbeth's freedom and happiness, but, perhaps merely because of the different mood of the denouement, he lacks the ruthless efficiency that makes Claudio seem like a humorous version of the menacing Cardinal Cibo in *Lorenzaccio.* Whenever the prince and his valet appear on stage, they present again a picture of ludicrous silliness and pomposity, lack of judgment, exaggerated insistence on elaborate protocol, and vanity of every sort, including the prince's belief that he has it in him to be the ideal Romantic lover. They may be closely related to Claudio and Tibia, but they are easily distinguishable from them, and the priests Blazius and Bridaine present yet another variation, perhaps the most successful of all.

This time they are a harmless, wholly comic pair, rivaling each other in girth and good living, pedantry and ignorance, and contrasting superbly with the gaunt and vinegarish Dame Pluche. In a masterpiece of witty caricature drawing the Chorus itemizes their shared characteristics of figure and personality, ending with a fine climax of description: "Already I can see them with their elbows propped on the table, their cheeks crimson, their eyes popping out of their heads, their triple chins quivering with hatred. They look each other over from head to foot, they begin with a few light skirmishes; soon war is declared, they exchange a cross-fire of abuse of all sorts and, to complete the unhappy scene, Dame Pluche fidgets between the two drunkards, keeping them both at bay with her bony elbows" (Act I, scene iii). Their dialogue is as amusing as their appearance, giving such passages as Blazius' extravaganza of drunken buffoonery, pedantry, and would-be cunning which conceals nothing (Act II, scene iv).

In between the boisterous, sometimes Falstaff-like grotesques and the young heroes and heroines there moves an intermediate group of characters, some semigrotesque and sympathetic at the same time, others presented with complete seriousness. David Sices, in his article "Musset's *Fantasio:* The Paradise of Chance" *(The Romantic Review,* LVIII [1967], 23-37), suggests the label of "les banals" for some of these figures, and this is certainly apt for the example he is considering—Elsbeth's governess, who dotes on her charge as the nurse in *Romeo and Juliet* does, and who almost joins the ranks of the grotesques by the way in which her speech is crammed with platitudes and novelettish fancies. Yet others seem to deserve better than to be classed as "banals." They share to some extent the sensitivity of the major characters over whose fortunes they watch solicitously. Some are parents, such as Elsbeth's father and the mothers of Coelio and Lorenzaccio, whose tender concern reflects Musset's own relationship with his mother. Carmosine's parents again contrive to be both amusing and touching, occasionally amusing in their run-of-the-mill domestic arguments and yet pathetic in their grief and affection for their daughter.

Even those characters who are on stage only briefly have definite personalities which are rapidly but firmly established. For instance, Cesario, André del Sarto's apprentice, quickly reveals his superficial attitude toward art and his shallow, pleasure-seeking nature, yet his role is a very minor one. Perhaps Hermia in *Les Caprices de Marianne* is the most poetic of these characters who are painted in comparatively subdued colors and placed in the middle ground of the drama, but for me the most impressive of these supporting parts is that of Spark, Fantasio's confidant. In most ways he is the complete antithesis of Fantasio, and he throws into relief his friend's will-o'-the-wisp mind with his own stolid, prudent, pipe-smoking presence. Quick with offers of practical help, he can nevertheless be impatient with and critical of Fantasio's wilder flights of fancy and his introspection. Fantasio longs to escape from himself into exotic fantasy; Spark is perfectly content with the commonplace. "As for me, when I smoke, for instance, my thoughts become tobacco smoke; when I drink, they turn into Spanish wine or Flemish beer; when I kiss my mistress's hand, they make their way through her slender fingertips and race on electric currents all through her being" (Act I, scene ii). Throughout, he presents the common-sense counterpart to Fantasio's cynicism and restlessness, but as far as intellect is concerned he is on a par with his friend and he too is articulate. "What you say would make many people laugh," he comments when Fantasio describes his despair at the limitations of a human being's existence, "but it makes me shudder: there lies the history of the whole century. Eternity is a huge eyrie, from which all the centuries, like eaglets, have in their turn flown away across the sky and out of sight; ours in its turn has reached the edge of its nest; but its wings have been clipped, and it waits for death, gazing at the space into which it cannot take flight." Spark is an admirable foil for the hero, but he has an important viewpoint of his own to express, and he is enough of a match for Fantasio to make their friendship seem natural, unlike those forced antitheses found in some Romantic works.

VII *Heroines*

When the reader turns his attention to the heroines and compares them with the majority of those on the Romantic stage, he realizes why Musset has been classed with Racine and Marivaux for his understanding of the way a woman's mind works. Hugo's Doña Sol, Queen

Maria, and Régina are beautiful and often moving creatures, but at times one feels that they are no more than splendidly designed dolls through whose mouths Hugo pours his poetry of love, dignity, and pathos. It is difficult to imagine them passing that stringent test of character creation, the ability to live outside the work which gave them being, as Don Juan, Faust, and Figaro succeed in doing. Vigny's Kitty Bell in *Chatterton* seems to me more a creature of flesh and blood, but even she cannot compare with Marianne, Elsbeth, or Camille for lifelike complexity. The stereotyped Romantic heroine, before Carmen and her fellow *femmes fatales* arrive on the scene, is an angelic, white-robed creature mounted high on a pedestal of idealization, but Musset is not afraid to make his Marianne and Camille convincingly and realistically disagreeable at times and to describe them in unflattering terms which it is impossible to imagine one of Hugo's heroes using. "She is a skinny doll, endlessly mumbling her 'Aves'," says Octave of Marianne.

Even in trivial touches, a woman reader may recognize how well Musset understood her sex. In *Louison* the Maréchale urges her daughter-in-law to try on her new ball gown, although she has no heart to go to the ball. "Sometimes merely changing one's dress can make one change one's mind" (Act I, scene viii). All his full-length portraits of young girls or young women are worth studying in detail and, although some of them leave a general impression of ethereal delicacy in the mind as though they might disintegrate like a butterfly's wing if they were touched, close examination shows that they are in fact real members of the human race. Carmosine, by the very nature of her role of passive grief, is one of the palest heroines, but to me at least she seems credible, combining pathos with dignity in a part which could have easily turned her into one of the worst examples of lachrymose, self-pitying despair in the manner of the second-rate Romantics. André del Sarto's wife would have fitted just as easily into a stereotype—that of the young, luxury-loving wife wooed away from her husband by a determined lover. Yet Musset, in the few moments when he shows her alone on the stage, adds depth by depicting her as a woman of religious beliefs, agonizingly torn between loyalty to her husband and the need to save her lover, as she sees it, by assuring his happiness even at the expense of destroying herself spiritually.

I can think of no heroine in the *Comédies et Proverbes* who does not ring true, but probably the most complex studies are those of Marianne, Elsbeth, and Camille. It is surprising that Elsbeth, the slightest sketch of the three, should have any substance at all, for she seems typecast by the plot as the fairy-tale princess who is rescued by the mysterious stranger from unhappy marriage. The flower-garden setting in which she meets Fantasio, his lyrical description of her weeping as she stands before the mirror in her bridal array—these touches heighten the fairy-tale aura around her—but despite this, a clearly defined personality emerges. She is far more of a realist than her governess, recognizing and accepting the facts about her loutish fiancé and the course of action her sense of political duty and loyalty to her father require of her. She reveals her intelligence not only in her philosophical battle of repartee with Fantasio but also in her self-analysis. She realizes that she knows little of the world and that she has been brought up on a diet of novelettes which have prepared her better for daydreaming than for reality. She is skeptical about the miraculous intervention her governess expects. Indeed, in a levelheaded way completely untypical of Romantic heroines destined to a loveless match, she does not wallow in despair, but manages to persuade herself that she may find happiness of a sort, even if of the most superficial kind, included among her wedding presents.

Elsbeth can conduct herself with royal dignity when the new jester grows too impertinent, but, like the ideal of womanhood described by Fantasio in Act I, scene ii, she is "as gentle as the West wind" compared with Marianne. During the latter's first few appearances on stage, as we saw before, the tartness of her replies, her prickly virtue, and her hauteur make the audience share Octave's original opinion of her, despite her beauty. It is only when his jibes have opened up the oyster shell of her beliefs and feelings that we can sympathize with her, and realize that her apparent contrariness toward the end of the play is caused partly by her violent and understandable sense of outraged self-respect at Claudio's treatment of her, and partly by her attempt to win Octave as her lover without actually having to admit that he attracts her. In sending as fascinating an advocate as Octave, Coelio had in fact been "playing with love" and with the happiness of three people just as much as Camille and Perdican do in *On ne badine pas avec l'amour.*

Camille is by far the most complex of the three girls, and it is worth while to trace the gradual revelation and development of her attitudes during the course of the play. Her very first words and actions indicate the lines of conduct she will follow in the early part of the play—her refusal of a kiss of greeting, her priggish moralizing ("Neither friendship nor love should accept anything which they cannot return"), her admiring pause before the portrait of an ancestress who was a nun—all these lead us to believe by the end of the second scene that her education has spoiled her nature as Perdican's has not, that she has been turned into a "spotless dove" from Dame Pluche's standpoint (Act II, scene i) and from Perdican's into one of those "pale statues carved by the nuns, who have their head where their heart should be, and who when they leave the cloisters spread the dank atmosphere of their cells all around them" (Act III, scene iii). At her second appearance she is as abrupt and haughty as Marianne, ungraciously turning her back on memories of pre-convent-school days, but at the beginning of Act II her feelings are shown to be more complex than she would have anyone believe. She announces her decision not to marry in a language so firm and direct as to be almost martial, but her stung pride at Perdican's easy acceptance of her refusal is very different from the humility one would expect of a "spotless dove," and at the end of scene i her conversation with Dame Pluche reveals that she is far from having a clear picture of her future role in life. "Am I not to be his wife? I can surely write to my fiancé."

The sight of Perdican flirting with Rosette cracks the ice of her feelings, and a scene as crucial as Marianne's interview with Octave outside the inn opens with her sitting among the daisies at the fountain's edge, putting her hand in Perdican's and giving him the kiss she had refused before. Now the reader has to be constantly on the alert to catch every nuance of what the dialogue has to tell about Camille. Why does she now ask Perdican's opinion about whether she is doing right to become a nun when she seemed so unshakable in her resolve before? Could it be pride again which would like to hear him pleading with her to change her mind? or does a part of her almost hope that his persuading will succeed? The burst of questions she fires at Perdican about his past relations with women seems strangely abrupt and direct too, until one realizes that all her knowledge of men is secondhand, that this is the crucial factor in her intention to reject the world, and that she is urgently trying to test the truth of what she has been told by measuring it against Perdican. She shows the same critical intelligence as Marianne and Elsbeth. "If your parish priest breathed on you, and told me that you would love me all your life, would I be right to believe him?"

The somber tale unfolds of the imaginary life she created for herself while in the convent, torn between the warnings of those who had been deceived by the world and her dreams of the imaginary lover who had the features of Perdican, her childhood sweetheart ("Truly, I have loved you, Perdican"). She is aware that her ideas have been learned parrot-fashion and may be wrong, but she is too afraid of the sufferings of human love to risk testing them by experience. There is an unattractive pride in her condescending advice to Perdican to forget her unless he ever comes to despair, when he may think of her praying for him, and vanity in her own beauty plays an important part in her pleasurable anticipation of the dramatic side of the ceremony at which she will take the veil. Yet sometimes there is a note of desperation and sincerity in her words (she is, after all, modeled to some extent on George Sand's experience of convent school) which wins the reader's sympathy, a note which makes this previously cold and assured girl sound young and frightened: "I was wrong to say anything; my whole life is on my lips. Oh Perdican! do not laugh at me; all this is desperately sad."

In the following scenes she swings between coldness and coquetry until the baffled Perdican compares her to a jewel that changes color with each ray of sunlight (Act III, scene vi), but each fresh piece of apparent capriciousness develops logically the study of the conflict raging inside her. Her pride, self-dramatization, and deceitfulness show clearly enough that her devoutness is not more than skin deep, yet her frantic despair when it seems that Perdican will indeed marry Rosette, and the sincerity and turmoil of mind in her prayer at the beginning of the final scene prove that her dilemma is not a part of her posing but is quite real.

Compared with this passionate temperament led by an unhealthy upbringing to cause tragedy to itself and others, Rosette with her good sense and simplicity reflects Musset's ideal of girlhood, the "wild flower" instead of the hothouse plant, and the more detailed portrait of Cécile in *Il ne faut jurer de rien* shows that he did not think that this happy state need be restricted to the peasantry. Cécile may perhaps make less impact on the reader than Marianne and Camille with their tortured natures, but she surely comes closer to Musset's blueprint of perfection, with her honesty, candor, compassion, and innocence, coupled with sharp intelligence, and to crown it all a sense of the poetic. It was Marianne, however, rather than Cécile, whom Musset described as being womanhood incarnate. The elder sisters in this theater, the witty and wise young Parisian widows such as Madame de Léry *(Un Caprice)* and the Marchioness in *Il faut qu'une porte soit ouverte ou fermée* are just as attractive, and indeed the greatest problem about studying Musset's heroines, apart from the awareness of failing to do them justice, is the difficulty of leaving them for other subjects.

VIII *Heroes*

It might be inferred that Musset's portraits of young men are less original and are on a slightly lower plane because most of them reflect at least some facets of his own character and experience of life. The very fact that they do so gives them value beyond the dimensions of the plays which contain them and certainly saves them from joining the ranks of those cliché-ridden, improbable heroes who bear little relation to their author or to any other human being outside the Romantic dreamworld. Nevertheless, by incorporating some of Musset's feelings and problems, they throw a powerful beam of light on the Romantic generation as a whole. In particular, in Act I, scene ii of *Fantasio,* the dialogue between the hero and Spark is worth rereading time and again as a brilliant illustration of the young men analyzed in the second chapter of *La Confession d'un enfant du siècle.*

Valuable as the heroes are as biographical or social documents, it would be unthinkable for a dramatist of Musset's caliber merely to produce a carbon copy of himself in each play, and a glance at some of his leading men will show, I believe, that the most important of them are fragments of his own personality turned into beings with an independent existence of their own and as varied and distinct from each other as their female counterparts. If it were not too fanciful to imagine meeting these beings outside the context of the *Comédies et Proverbes,* the experiment would show that it would be impossible to take Perdican for Coelio, or to think that Fantasio and Lorenzaccio bore a closer resemblance to each other than that which might be expected between younger and elder brother. Indeed, it is true that there is a strong family resemblance between most of the heroes. All are intelligent and self-analytical; most are witty; and, apart from André del Sarto and perhaps the Count in *Il faut qu'une porte soit ouverte ou fermée,* even the most world-weary of them is as young in years as his creator was.

Not surprisingly, Razetta, one of the two heroes of *La Nuit vénitienne,* still has some of the extravagant Romantic panache of the young gallants of the *Premières Poésies,* with his flamboyant gambling, his melodramatic despair and threat of suicide. Yet his cynicism and disillusionment with the world in general turn him into an interesting embryo of Lorenzaccio, and the Prince of Eysenach, Razetta's co-hero, who like him is bored and sunk in an apathy which others label laziness, fanciful in his views on finding a bride and treating her once she is found with extraordinary understanding, tenderness, and gallantry, shows in sketch form the lines along which later heroes would develop.

In some ways André del Sarto, the first full-length study, seems less close to Musset than these two characters and later ones. From the first he is a sympathetic figure, full of warm friendship and concern for Cordiani, and later in the play he takes on the impressive stature of the hero in a Spanish play of honor, bearing himself with grim patience and self-control even when he reaches the point of despair. Rather than a reflection of Musset, he seems like the author's forecast of what might conceivably be his own life-story, for André is torn between the claims of art and those of life. The one thing that binds him to life, which had otherwise disappointed him, is the presence of the woman he loves, and when she leaves the very mainspring of his existence is broken.

Octave and Coelio are justly well known as the two halves of Musset's nature, opposites whom he sets together on the stage until—prophetically—the cynical and debauched Octave is unwittingly instrumental in killing the idealistic Coelio. As antithetical as the figures in a child's weather house, they are nevertheless both attractive characters, except perhaps to those readers who cannot abide the poetic, melancholy, fatalistic lover whom Coelio represents, shy as the Musset who had to admit his love for George Sand in writing instead of to her face. Yet Octave in his summing-up speech before Coelio's tomb describes him as a potential man of action who would have braved death for his mistress as readily as he would have drawn his sword to avenge a murdered friend. It was he who was capable of true and lasting love, whereas Octave, the eternal reveler with his blasé wit, is little more than a husk from which his excesses have drained away all capacity for sustained feeling and all respect for women.

Opposite Camille, the most self-tortured of Musset's heroines, stands one of his most attractive young men and one who runs counter to most Romantic heroes in that he presents the picture of psychological health. By the end of the play Perdican has contributed to his own tragedy through lacking the wisdom to realize the dangers of tampering with another's emotions, but in the first scenes he seems the ideal young nobleman—unspoiled by his learning, showing affection for the scenes and acquaintances of his childhood, simple and modest, full of charm, gentleness, and warmth. Both Coelio and Octave are reflected in him. He has Coelio's ability—which Musset coveted so much for himself—to love deeply and lastingly. Yet there is a worldliness about him which seems to justify Camille's worst fears. He freely admits that he has had mistresses who now mean nothing to him; whether seriously or not, he advises Camille to take lovers if he should tire of her when they are married; and he has none of her belief in eternal life. Like Musset, his overriding belief is in the value of love itself, and his famous speech at the end of Act II probably places him second only to Lorenzaccio as Musset's most-quoted hero.

His role in the play is not that of the immovable advocate of love. Despite his apparent maturity in the opening scenes, his youthfulness betrays itself in the way in which he becomes caught up in a maelstrom of confused feelings. He is enough Musset's creature to show considerable understanding of women, but the walking contradiction that is Camille leaves him baffled for much of the play, both as to her true feelings and his own. In the explanatory scene by the fountain (Act II, scene v) Musset gives a masterly picture of his swiftly changing reactions to Camille's words—disgust, indignation, sympathy, and ardent statement of his own beliefs. Finally he becomes locked with Camille in a frantic duel of false pride which is resolved too late to save either Rosette's life or the couple's happiness.

To some it may seem a distortion to compare *Lorenzaccio* with a painting by Leonardo da Vinci or a Beethoven concerto, but for me Musset's masterpiece bears the stamp of true greatness which can cause a critic to approach it with mixed feelings of enthusiasm and hesitation, enthusiasm to discuss the qualities which give it stature, and hesitation at attempting to do justice in a short space to a subject which could not be exhausted in a large volume. The figure of Lorenzaccio himself towers over the theater in nineteenth-century France, but many of the supporting roles have a depth and detail which put them almost on a par with the leading roles in the rest of the *Comédies et Proverbes*. Don Salluste in Hugo's *Ruy Blas* is described by the author himself as Satan become grandee of Spain, but Musset is too much a fanatic for psychological truth to adopt Hugo's unmodified blacks and whites of character portrayal. Even Salviati, the scum of the Florentine court, is made to seem a little less vile by the explanation that his own wife's dishonor is such public knowledge that he tries to prove that all women are as light as she. The Duke himself, the villain of the play from the ideological standpoint, is shown as a callous, murderous lecher, but he has an attractive side. "You are as brave as you are handsome," says the Marquise de Cibo. "If you have done wrong, it is because you are young and headstrong. . . ." (Act III, scene vi). Cruel though he can be, he thinks the butchery of his reign, which has been dictated by his overlords, excessive (Act I, scene iv); he protects art and artists; at times he acts with an impressive dignity; and occasionally his humor gives a touch of lightness to the somber theme—he cannot take seriously, for instance, the Pope's fury over the statues beheaded by Lorenzaccio, "statues that he would excommunicate tomorrow if they were flesh and blood" (*loc. cit.*).

The Cardinal, whose sinister, all-seeing figure broods in the background of the play, like a "bald-headed vulture," comes far closer to complete villainy, but the historical and indeed universal truth of such manipulators of men and events makes it impossible to compare him to the unreal figures of the contemporary melodrama. Nor, at the other end of the moral scale, is Philippe Strozzi unreal. In the interests of providing a dramatic contrast with the hero, Musset makes him more of a noble idealist than history warranted, but he shows too how his pure idealism could not make the transition into effective action, whereas Lorenzo, corrupt and cynical though he was, moved relentlessly ahead with his preparations for the political murder of the tyrant. Above all, Philippe is human in his frenzy of grief for his children. Already in *André del Sarto* Musset had shown how convincingly he could reproduce the voice of a man almost demented by sorrow.

The character of Lorenzo himself unfolds with the fascinating precision of the speeded-up film of a flower's opening. In the early scenes it is the vile aspects of his nature, those which form his fellow citizens' image of him, that are presented to us. His very first speech shows him as a loathsome corrupter. At his second appearance, a silent one, we see him as a drunken, blasphemous brawler, dressed as a nun and hurling a broken bottle from a window. Yet, says the Provéditeur, for all his pranks, he has hardly ever been seen to smile (Act I, scene ii). In scene iv, Sire Maurice takes up the somber description. Lorenzo is an atheist who jeers at everything, the Duke's pander. The Duke himself, for all his friendship for Lorenzo, paints the unflattering portrait of a cowardly, effeminate dreamer; a weakling undermined by his excesses, lacking the strength even to turn his occasional smile into a laugh. We learn that, as the Duke's spy, he betrays his fellow citizens, and scene iv ends with the ignominy of "dear Lorenzetta" being carried away swooning at the sight of a drawn sword.

Two scenes later, his mother and his aunt complete the physical description for the armchair audience—Lorenzo's dark eyes, his cheeks the color of sulphur, his habitually sneering expression—and underline the mystery surrounding him. "He is still handsome sometimes in his strange melancholy." From them too we learn of his earlier years, when his nobility of birth and nature, his intellect and good looks all seemed to promise a brilliant future. So, by the end of Act I, we have the full picture of a depraved wreck of a man, but as yet no key to the explanation of what has happened to him and no means of knowing that this most unheroic hero will do his utmost to free his city from tyranny.

Act II begins to suggest that there is more to Lorenzo than degradation. In scene iv we see him in his home, cynical still but strangely moved by his mother's hallucinatory vision of his earlier self. Trembling from head to foot, he begs Catherine to read the story of Brutus. After the witty interlude with Bindo which shows how closely he is related to Octave and Fantasio, Lorenzo tries to deflect the Duke's interest away from his aunt, proving that he is not the complete incarnation of corruption suggested earlier. Then follow two incidents showing how preparations for the Duke's murder fill his mind. When Pierre Strozzi returns from attacking Salviati, Lorenzo's admiration of him is significant; "You are splendid, Pierre, as great as vengeance," and he draws him aside to ask exactly how the assault was carried out and where he struck his victim (Act II, scene v).

Next he steals the Duke's protective coat of mail, and in Act III, scene i he is systematically accustoming his neighbors to the sound of uproar in his room. Scoronconcolo's description of his fighting, comparing him to a tiger and his roars to a cave full of panthers and lions, is bafflingly different from his womanish faint earlier. In an almost delirious transport he speaks of his vengeance: "Oh day of blood, my wedding day!"—and grieves over the sufferings of the city at the Duke's hands, using broken phrases which read like rhapsodic twentieth-century verse: "Farewells, endless farewells, the banks of the Arno full of farewells!" This man is a complete contrast with the emotionless reprobate of Act I, and at last, in Act III, scene iii, the explanation of his behavior bursts from him in the dialogue with Philippe Strozzi which is the keystone of the play. The distraught Philippe begs Lorenzaccio the actor to lay aside his vile mask and reveal his true nature. "When the stones cried out as you passed, when your every step made a pool of human blood spurt up, I called you by the sacred name of friend, I stopped my ears in order to believe you, I shut my eyes in order to love you." To the reader's surprise, Philippe calls Lorenzo "an unshakable man," unlike himself; and under his pressure Lorenzo first explains his melancholy, "beside which the blackest night is a dazzling light," then clarifies the course of the action by making a firm statement that he will murder the Duke in the next day or two.

The complete opposite of the usual verbose Romantic hero, he is laconic in his replies to Philippe's probing until finally he is spurred on into revealing why men should beware of the "demon who whispers of liberty." Now we see how far down the roots of his cynicism strike. "Take care, Philippe, you have given thought to the happiness of mankind." The moment which began his transformation from a peaceful, studious youth, "as pure as gold," to the Duke's companion in debauchery is the quintessence of Romanticism. "Suddenly, one night when I was sitting among the ruins of the ancient Coliseum, I stood up—I do not know why, lifted my arms wet with dew toward the sky, and swore that one of the tyrants of my country should die by my hand." Love of humanity was one of his motives, but so too was pride, which dictated that his murder bid must be a solo performance and so led him further and further into the vicious ways of the tyrant whose confidant he must pretend to be. Ironically, this path led him to see all the failings of that humanity for which he was working and showed him that his heroism would be useless, for his fellow citizens would be too weak or too indifferent to seize the chance which he offered them to shake off despotic rule. Nor would he be able to resume his peaceful, virtuous existence after the murder, for he had seen too much of the baser aspects of mankind to forget what he had learned, and the disguise of depravity had now stuck to his skin.

He was still driving himself on to complete the task that would achieve nothing—*l'acte gratuit* of Existentialist philosophers—for it formed his only link with his former self; "my whole life is at the tip of my dagger." Pride, too, the princely pride of a member of the Medici family, must be satisfied. "Men must realize something of who I am and who they are. . . . Whether men understand or not, whether they act or not, I shall have said all that I have to say. . . . In two days, mankind will appear before the tribunal of my will." Idealist turned cynic, proud, solitary, and feeling himself superior to the masses, Lorenzaccio is the acme of the Romantic hero, but free from the most typical of his exaggerations.

After this crucial scene, the action speeds on to the denouement which Lorenzaccio has foretold. We see him completing his plans, paying the additional price of wrecking his mother's health with grief, and only just preventing himself from trying to corrupt his young aunt herself. Again and again he returns in wonderment to the theme of the strange, perhaps divine fire that has taken possession of him, driving him on to murder a man who has been kind to him, and turning him from a love of flowers, meadows, and Petrarch's sonnets to a fierce blood lust (Act IV, scenes iii and v). The fire burns up to a frenzy in the last minutes of preparation; then for a brief moment Lorenzaccio can lapse into an ecstasy of joy, gazing out into the Florentine night as his victim lies dead in the room behind him.

The last act, in a chilling coda, completes what he has forecast. In his exile his cynicism remains and his gloom is intensified now that his aim is accomplished. "I am more hollow and emptier than a tin statue. . . . I am older than Saturn's great-grandfather." His enjoyment of wine and women is strong enough to keep him a debauchee, but not strong enough to make him content to be one. His mother dies, the city of Florence is failing to seize the chance he dedicated himself to securing for it, and in one final act of hostility the crowd throws his murdered body into a canal. Enigmatic, yet unfolding with ruthless inevitability, the essence of his time and yet a comparatively faithful historical portrait, the character of Lorenzaccio deserves to be bracketed, as it often is, with Shakespeare's Hamlet.

Seen as a whole, Musset's theater might well make the reader feel like acclaiming it, as Schumann did Chopin's work, with: "Hats off, gentlemen; a genius!"

CHAPTER 5

Conclusion

M ANY people will have experienced the disappointment caused by reading through the complete works of an author whose writings they had admired in anthologies, only to find that he was capable of producing many pages which seem mediocre in comparison with those they already knew. The reader who takes up a volume of Musset's complete writings rarely runs the risk of such an anticlimax. It is true that the Romantic clichés of *La Quittance du Diable* and one or two very early poems such as *Agnès* are unlikely to do more than cause amusement nowadays and that, toward the other end of his career, the verse of *Louison* seems dreary in comparison with the sparkle of his plays in prose. It is true too that, while Musset's journalism is brilliant, his short stories rarely seem to rise above the level of elegant, often charming competence. Yet these exceptions are few, and most of his works, far from being fodder suitable for adolescence alone, yield more riches, whether of content or technique, on each rereading. Musset paid a high price, both financially and in the reproaches of laziness which were heaped on him, for the artistic integrity which made him wait for inspiration before setting pen to paper. His posthumous reward was the stamp of distinction borne by almost everything he wrote. It is only a tantalizingly promising fragment such as *Faustine* which makes one wish that he had been less easily distracted from his writing table.

It is clear that the world found in his works is a restricted one, though less restricted, I think, than people who know him only through his most-quoted poems would believe. This is not necessarily adverse criticism, for an exquisite Delius tone poem is none the less fine for not being a massive Beethoven symphony, nor a miniature for not being on the scale of a vast fresco. One boundary is imposed by the fact that Musset rarely chose subjects which did not in some way echo his own preoccupations. It would be unfair automatically to draw the conclusion that he had not a truly creative imagination, for his plays show

how he could enter into the skin of characters very different from himself. Nevertheless, the result is that his world is dominated by the young and by the typical concerns of youth. This might tempt readers to think of him as a literary Peter Pan if they did not remember how astonishingly young he was when he wrote his masterpieces. By the time a man might be expected to expatiate on other great themes of life besides love, physical and psychological ill-health had almost silenced Musset. His favorite theme—that of young men and women striving to cope with their circumstances, their relationships with other people, and their own natures—he handles with such perception that in his hands it becomes a tool, narrow but diamond-pointed, which penetrates to the heart of life.

Like Chopin, who shared his feelings for George Sand, Musset expresses himself most often in comparatively small-scale works, although *Lorenzaccio* proves how successfully he could treat a vast theme. Perhaps partly because of this choice of sphere, both he and Chopin have suffered from the quite mistaken general impression that their works lack power. Nevertheless it is true that the most characteristic sound of both artists is formed by the harmonizing of delicacy, poetry, and gaiety. Musset's universe is exquisite, inspiring critics to lyricism themselves. It is a land, writes Doumic, where the days are bathed in a golden mist, where the balmy nights bring sweet-scented breezes, where everything helps to form a perfect setting for love.[1] It is a magical dream, says des Essarts, in a setting filled with music, the scent of flowers, and moonlight. "The strains of the waltz intertwine with the conversations of *La Porte ouverte,* of *Un Caprice,* of *Il ne faut jurer de rien;* the sparkling laughter of Fantasio, Octave and Valentin blends with the orchestra's harmonies; while in the shade and along the walks the solitary voices of Coelio, Rosette, Fortunio and Carmosine speak of their sad love, and in the far distance, at the loneliest place in the park, the tragic image of Lorenzaccio rises on its marble pedestal, white against the blue night-sky."[2]

This landscape might well be a painting by Watteau, and there are many analogies that Musset's writings bring to mind. He has been compared from some angles with Racine and with Watteau's contemporary, Marivaux; there are moments when he brings to mind Keats, Byron, and Rubén Darío. As far as the influence of other writers on him is concerned, a man who cared as much for literature as he did inevitably found help at times in other works, whether in making a definite borrowing (of images from Hoffmann, or plots from Boccaccio and Bandello, for instance), or in learning more general lessons of theatercraft from Shakespeare or style from La Fontaine. In spite of this, no one author seems to have had a direct and widespread influence on Musset, intent as he was on transcribing the sounds of his own individual voice.

On the other hand, no writer springs immediately to mind as an obvious heir to Musset. Sometimes a flight of fantasy in Giraudoux, the atmosphere of a Maeterlinck play brings him to mind, but never for long. One reason may be the difficulty of successfully imitating a genius whose nature was as elusive as the personality of its possessor, but probably literary fashion too was partly responsible through its rejection of the Romantics, which began before Musset's death and is still continuing. It is ironical that, after he had been blamed by the Romantic group and the public during his lifetime for going his own independent way, his reputation should have suffered, together with those of the men with whom he had parted company, from the reaction against what was looked on as oversentimentality and overlushness. From Baudelaire to Gide, later writers tended to speak of Musset's work in the most derisive terms as an outmoded drawing-room ornament, as material fit to be read only by empty-headed girls. It is certain that the Symbolists and later poets still would have been horrified to think that they owed anything to him, and it is highly unlikely that any of them ever consciously took his technique as a model. Nevertheless, listening to the voice of his Muse as later poets listened to what was now called the subconscious, Musset hit on a way of writing poetry which was to develop more and more in modern times. His mind leaps from idea to idea, image to image almost too quickly to provide his reader with the logical links between them. "His images are like swiftly passing hallucinations," comments Van Tieghem, "like instantaneous 'illuminations' which the poet has not time to 'explain' but which suggest a complete picture, sometimes a complete symbolical scene."[3]

As far as his reputation outside France is concerned, Musset does not export as easily as an author whose chief stock-in-trade consists of ideas or stories. The poetic and the natural combine in his style with such a delicacy that, just as mimosa from southern French hillsides easily loses its feathery texture when it is sent overseas, Musset's works find it very difficult to survive translation. Yet, although his world reputation must depend largely on his being read in the original, I believe that, in his restricted sphere, he reaches an artistic greatness which need bow to none.

The world he creates cannot be to everyone's taste. Some feel confined within his bounds, needing wider horizons and a greater range of characters and emotions. Others prefer to find psychological truth in a starker setting, in a tenement rather than in an idealized Ile-de-France, although it is worth remembering that Shakespeare himself returned to fantasy in *The Tempest,* one of his last and greatest plays. Yet, leaving aside those people who are intellectually allergic to Musset as some are to Tschaikowsky, I believe that many more readers could find enjoyment in him if they could approach him without having to penetrate the barrage of jeering which, in Great Britain at least, still often surrounds the Romantics. In one sense, it is fair that Musset has been grouped with the school which he abandoned, for intrinsically his work belongs very much to its period. But I have tried to show how his mature work rid itself of nearly all the exaggerations and all the overflamboyance of some of his contemporaries. His appreciative audience would increase too if students of French would no longer think of him exclusively as the creator of a moonlit garden where a poet with a lute in his hand stood communing with his muse. In his writings and in his life, there is an open-eyed encounter with problems as commonly met with in twentieth-century skyscraper apartments as in nineteenth-century country houses. His compassionate, perceptive studies of men and women give his work greatness from the human point of view; from the esthetic point of view, his writings have a grace, fantasy, wit, and poetry which have rarely been rivaled.

Notes and References

Chapter One

1. Madame Martellet, née Adèle Colin, *Dix ans chez Alfred de Musset* (Paris, 1899), p. 89. See also p. 185: "Il avait tant besoin qu'on l'aime! on aurait cru qu'il ne vivait que pour ça."

2. Philippe Soupault, *Alfred de Musset,* Collection Poètes d'aujourd'hui (Paris, 1957); see pp. 9-11.

3. *Correspondance d'Alfred de Musset, 1827-1857,* ed. Léon Séché, 2nd ed. (Paris, 1907), letter CII (June, 1840), p. 164.

4. J.-A. Barbey d'Aurevilly, *Poésies et Poètes,* 3rd ed. (Paris, 1906), p. 284.

5. Emile Henriot, *Alfred de Musset,* Collection Les Romantiques (Paris, 1928), pp. 103 and 107.

6. For descriptions of Musset's appearance as a young man see Maurice Donnay, *Musset et l'amour,* Collection Hier et Aujourd'hui (Paris, 1926), p. 11; and Léon Séché, *Etudes d'histoire romantique. Alfred de Musset* (Paris, 1907), vol. I, p. 72.

7. Juste Olivier, *Souvenirs* (Paris, 1830), p. 14.

8. This sketch, belonging to the Lardin de Musset collection, is reproduced in Maurice Allem's *Alfred de Musset,* revised edition (Grenoble–Paris, 1948), facing p. 13.

9. John Charpentier, *Alfred de Musset* (Paris, 1938), p. 9.

10. Pierre Gastinel, *Le Romantisme d'Alfred de Musset* (Paris, 1933), p. 70.

11. Letter LXXXIX, Oct. 27, 1837. Unless otherwise stated, all references to Musset's letters give the number they bear in Séché's edition of his correspondence; see note 3 above.

12. Gastinel, p. 163.

13. *Correspondance de Victor de Musset avec M. de Cayrol, critique de L'Universel.* Quoted by Gastinel, p. 148.

14. André Maurois, *Lélia, ou la vie de George Sand* (Paris, 1952), p. 182.

15. André Lebois, *Vues sur le théâtre de Musset* (Avignon, 1966), pp. 8-11.

16. Jean Pommier, *Variétés sur Alfred de Musset et son théâtre. Musset et George Sand. Musset et la Princesse Belgiojoso* (Paris, 1966), p. 55.

17. Donnay, p. 41.

18. See Charles Maurras, *Les Amants de Venise,* new ed. (Paris, 1916), for a detailed analysis of the personalities of George Sand and Musset.

19. Quoted by Soupault, p. 18.

20. Séché, vol. II, p. 183.

Notes and References

21. *Lettres d'amour à Aimée d'Alton,* ed. Léon Séché (Paris, 1910), No. II, pp. 58-59.
22. *Ibid.,* no. XXXIX, p. 136.

Chapter Two

1. See André von Mandach, "Eine wiedergefundene Novelle von Alfred de Musset: 'Les Amours du petit Job et de la belle Blandine,' Okt. 1856," *Zeitschrift für französische Sprache und Literatur,* LXXVII, 4 (July, 1967), 347-59.

Chapter Three

1. Lines 48-55:
   O ma fleur! ô mon immortelle!
   Seul être pudique et fidèle
   Où vive encor l'amour de moi!
   Oui, te voilà, c'est toi, ma blonde,
   C'est toi, ma maîtresse et ma sœur!
   Et je sens, dans la nuit profonde,
   De ta robe d'or qui m'inonde
   Les rayons glisser dans mon cœur.
2. Robert Graves, *Oxford Addresses on Poetry* (London, 1961), p. 59.
3. Lines 12-17, 22-24:
   Au moment du travail, chaque nerf, chaque fibre
   Tressaille comme un luth que l'on vient d'accorder.
   On n'écrit pas un mot que tout l'être ne vibre.
   (Soit dit sans vanité, c'est ce que l'on ressent.)
   On ne travaille pas,—on écoute,—on attend.
   C'est comme un inconnu qui vous parle à voix basse.
   . . . .
   Et puis,—et puis,—enfin!—on a mal à la tête.
   Quel étrange réveil!—comme on se sent boiteux!
   Comme on voit que Vulcain vient de tomber des cieux!
4. Stanza v:
   Vive le vieux roman, vive la page heureuse
   Que tourne sur la mousse une belle amoureuse!
   Vive d'un doigt coquet le livre déchiré,
   Qu'arrose dans le bain le robinet doré!
   Et, que tous les pédants frappent leur tête creuse,
   Vive le mélodrame où Margot a pleuré.
5. Lines 100-102:
   J'ai fait de mauvais vers, c'est vrai; mais, Dieu merci!
   Lorsque je les ai faits je les voulais ainsi,
   Et de Wailly ni Boiste, au moins, n'en sont la cause.
6. Lines 151-52:
   Les plus désespérés sont les chants les plus beaux,
   Et j'en sais d'immortels qui sont de purs sanglots.
7. Lines 54-56: . . . céleste, harmonieux langage,

Idiome de l'amour, si doux ou'à le parler
Tes femmes sur la lèvre en gardent un sourire.

8. Line 82:
Mon verre n'est pas grand, mais je bois dans mon verre.

9. Lines 161-66 and 171-75:
Vous me demanderez si j'aime quelque chose.
Je m'en vais vous répondre à peu près comme Hamlet:
Doutez, Ophélia, de tout ce qui vous plaît,
De la clarté des cieux, du parfum de la rose;
Doutez de la vertu, de la nuit et du jour;
Doutez de tout au monde, et jamais de l'amour.
. . . .
Doutez, si vous voulez, de l'être qui vous aime,
D'une femme ou d'un chien, mais non de l'amour même.
L'amour est tout,—l'amour, et la vie au soleil.
Aimer est le grand point, qu'importe la maîtresse?
Qu'importe le flacon, pourvu qu'on ait l'ivresse?

10. Lines 13-14:
. . . le sentier vert où, durant cette vie,
En se parlant tout bas, ils souriaient entre eux.

11. Lines 3-4:
Les bonbons, l'Océan, le jeu, l'azur des cieux,
Les femmes, les chevaux, les lauriers et les roses.

12. Lines 107-12:
Enfant par hasard adopté
    Et gâté,

Je brochais des ballades, l'une
    A la lune,
L'autre à deux yeux noirs et jaloux,
    Andaloux.

13. Lines 53-56:
Et qui, dans l'Italie,
    N'a son grain de folie?
Qui ne garde aux amours
    Ses plus beaux jours?

14. See the last three lines:
J'ai tué mon ami, j'ai mérité le feu,
J'ai taché mon pourpoint, et l'on me congédie.
C'est la moralité de cette comédie.

15. Canto iv, ll. 51-56:
Mais à peine au château quelques clartés encore
S'agitent çà et là.—Le silence,—l'effroi.—
Quelques pas, quelques sons traversent la nuit sombre;
Une porte a gémi dans un long corridor.—
Tiburce attend toujours.—Le ravisseur, dans l'ombre
N'a-t-il pas des pensers de meurtrier?—Tout dort.

16. Act IV, sc. i:
Voilà bien la sirène et la prostituée;—
Le type de l'égout;—la machine inventée

Pour désopiler l'homme et pour boire son sang;
La meule de pressoir de l'abrutissement.
Quelle atmosphère étrange on respire autour d'elle!
Elle épuise, elle tue, et n'en est que plus belle.
Deux anges destructeurs marchent à son côté;
Doux et cruels tous deux,—la mort,—la volupté.

17. I have left this line in the original French to avoid losing the effect described.

18. Lines 27-28:
Fière est cette forêt dans sa beauté tranquille,
Et fier aussi mon cœur.

19. *La Nuit d'août,* last stanza:
Dépouille devant tous l'orgueil qui te dévore,
Cœur gonflé d'amertume et qui t'es cru fermé.
Aime, et tu renaîtras; fais-toi fleur pour éclore.
Après avoir souffert, il faut souffrir encore;
Il faut aimer sans cesse, après avoir aimé.

20. Canto ii, ll. 125-30:
"Ciel et terre, Dalti! Nous sommes trois, dit-elle.
—Trois," répéta près d'eux une voix à laquelle
Répondirent au loin les voûtes du château.
Immobile, caché sous les plis d'un manteau,
Comme au seuil d'une porte une antique statue,
Onorio, debout, avait frappé leur vue.

21. This quotation and the next one have been left in the original French to avoid losing the effect to which reference is made.

Chapter Five

1. Quoted by Gastinel, pp. 335-36.
2. *Ibid.*
3. Philippe Van Tieghem, *Musset, l'homme et l'œuvre* (Paris, 1944), pp. 68-69.

Selected Bibliography

PRIMARY SOURCES

L'Anglais mangeur d'opium. Paris: Mame et Delaunay-Vallée, 1828.

Contes d'Espagne et d'Italie. Paris: Urbain Canel, 1830.

La Quittance du Diable. Written in 1830, this play was published only in 1914, by Maurice Allem in the *Revue Bleue.*

La Nuit vénitienne. Revue de Paris, December 1830.

Revues fantastiques. Le Temps, February 1 to June 6, 1831.

Un Spectacle dans un fauteuil. (La Coupe et les lèvres, A quoi rêvent les jeunes filles, Namouna). Paris: Renduel, 1833.

Le Roman par lettres. Written in 1833; first published in 1896.

André del Sarto. Revue des Deux Mondes (RDM), April 1, 1833.

Les Caprices de Marianne. RDM, May 15, 1833.

La Matinée de Don Juan (fragment). *La France littéraire,* December 1833.

Fantasio. RDM, January 1, 1834.

On ne badine pas avec l'amour. RDM, July 1, 1834.

Lorenzaccio. Published in *Un Spectacle dans un fauteuil,* seconde livraison, vol. I. Paris: Librairie de la *RDM,* 1834, 2 vols.

La Quenouille de Barberine. RDM, August 1, 1835.

Le Chandelier. RDM, November 1, 1835.

La Confession d'un enfant du siècle. Paris: Bonnaire, 1836, 2 vols.

Il ne faut jurer de rien. RDM, July 1, 1836.

Lettres de Dupuis et Cotonet. RDM, September 15, 1836, to May 15, 1837.

Un Caprice. RDM, June 15, 1837.

Emmeline. RDM, August 1, 1837.

Les Deux Maîtresses. RDM, November 1, 1837.

Frédéric et Bernerette. RDM, January 15, 1838.

Le Fils du Titien. RDM, May 1, 1838.

Margot. RDM, October 1, 1838.

Le Poète déchu. Written in 1839, but never published by Musset.

Croisilles. RDM, February 15, 1839.

Poésies nouvelles. First published as part of a volume entitled *Poésies complètes,* and including poems written since August, 1833. This volume was published in Paris in 1840. Many other poems were added to new editions of the *Poésies nouvelles* in 1850, 1851, and

Selected Bibliography

1852.
Histoire d'un merle blanc. Journal des débats, October 1842.
Pierre et Camille. Le Constitutionnel, April 16, 1843.
Le Secret de Javotte. Le Constitutionnel, June 18-22, 1844.
Les Frères Van Buck. Le Constitutionnel, July 27, 1844.
Il faut qu'une porte soit ouverte ou fermée. RDM, November 1, 1845.
Mimi Pinson. Published in a collection, *Le Diable à Paris,* December 20, 1845.
On ne saurait penser à tout. L'Ordre, June 1849.
Carmosine. Le Constitutionnel, November-December, 1850.
Bettine. RDM, November 1, 1851.
Louison. First published separately, then included in volume II of the *Comédies et Proverbes.* Paris: Charpentier, 1853.
La Mouche. Le Moniteur universel, December 23, 1853-January 6, 1854.
Les Amours du petit Job et de la belle Blandine. Gazette de la noblesse et des châteaux d'Europe, October 16, 1856. See André von Mandach, "Eine wiedergefundene Novelle von Alfred de Musset." *Zeitschrift für französische Sprache und Literatur,* LXXVII, 4 (July, 1967), 347-59.

Musset gave his final edition of his complete poetic works in 1854. In this edition, as in that of 1852, the *Contes d'Espagne et d'Italie* and the "première livraison" of the *Spectacle dans un fauteuil* are grouped together under the heading of *Premières Poésies.* The last edition of his plays to appear in his lifetime was published in 1856 as the two volumes of the *Comédies et Proverbes.* For a number of dramatic fragments not included in the above bibliography, and for a collection of poems not to be found in the *Premières Poésies* or the *Poésies nouvelles,* see Philippe van Tieghem's edition of Musset's *Œuvres complètes,* Collection L'Intégrale, Paris: Editions du Seuil, 1963.

SECONDARY SOURCES

ALLEM, MAURICE. *Alfred de Musset.* Grenoble-Paris: Arthaud, 1948.
This is the definitive edition of a valuable work by a well-known editor of Musset's works. Especially notable for some of its plates, for instance a photograph of Musset instead of the usual reproductions of portraits.
BARINE, ARVÈDE. *Alfred de Musset.* Paris: Hachette, 1893. An early book which benefited from its closeness to Musset's lifetime, and to which many later studies are indebted.
CHARPENTIER, JOHN. *Alfred de Musset.* Paris: Tallandier, 1938. A sympathetic and sensitive appreciation of Musset and his works.
DIMOFF, PAUL. *La Genèse de Lorenzaccio.* Paris: Droz, 1936. An

authoritative examination of the groundwork for Musset's greatest play.

DONNAY, MAURICE. *Musset et l'amour.* Paris: Flammarion, Collection Hier et Aujourd'hui, 1926. An interestingly written account of Musset's series of love affairs.

GASTINEL, PIERRE. *Le Romantisme d'Alfred de Musset.* Paris: Hachette, 1933. A masterly, exhaustive study of Musset's development as a man and writer.

GOCHBERG, HERBERT S. *Stage of Dreams. The Dramatic Art of Alfred de Musset (1828-1834).* Geneva: Droz, 1967. Examines the unfolding of Musset's dramatic gifts and especially his preoccupation with the theme of dreams versus reality.

HENRIOT, EMILE. *Alfred de Musset.* Paris: Hachette, Collection Les Romantiques, 1928. A valuable analysis, particularly of the impact Musset and his works made on his contemporaries.

LAFOSCADE, LÉON. *Le Théâtre d'Alfred de Musset.* Paris: Hachette, 1901. This work and that by Lefebvre listed below are two of the most useful studies of Musset's plays.

LEBOIS, ANDRÉ. *Vues sur le théâtre de Musset.* Avignon: Aubanel, 1966. The first of the three sections forming this book examines the roots from which *Lorenzaccio* sprang, and then gives a stimulating analysis of the play in detail.

LEFEBVRE, HENRI. *Alfred de Musset dramaturge.* Paris: l'Arche, Collection Les Grands Dramaturges, 1955. See under Lafoscade.

MARTELLET, ADÈLE. *Dix ans chez Alfred de Musset, par Mme Martellet, née A. Colin, sa gouvernante.* Paris: Chamuel, 1899. Musset's housekeeper tends to turn a blind eye to his faults, but her memoirs give a unique and fascinating account of his conduct of everyday affairs, and a sympathetic insight into the sufferings of his later years.

MAUROIS, ANDRÉ. *Lélia, ou la vie de George Sand.* Paris: Hachette, 1952. Gives an extremely readable account of Musset's relationship with George Sand.

MAURRAS, CHARLES. *Les Amants de Venise.* Paris: Flammarion, 1902. A penetrating study of this love affair, and of how it failed largely through factors inherent in the personalities of the two lovers and in the outlook of their period.

MUSSET, PAUL DE. *Biographie d'Alfred de Musset. Sa vie et ses œuvres.* Paris: Charpentier, 1877. Paul understandably whitewashes certain aspects of his life, but his biography is rich in interesting detail, especially of the brothers' childhood.

– – –. *Lui et elle.* Paris: Charpentier, 1860. A counterblast to George Sand's account of her relationship with Alfred.

POMMIER, JEAN. *Variétés sur Alfred de Musset et son théâtre.* Paris: Nizet, 1966. A probing examination of various topics.

———. *Autour du drame de Venise. G. Sand et A. de Musset au lendemain de "Lorenzaccio."* Paris: Nizet, 1958. Quotes evidence to prove that *Lorenzaccio* was written before Musset's visit to Italy and not afterward as had been supposed.

SAND, GEORGE. *Elle et lui. RDM,* January 15 to March 1, 1859. George's own account of her love affair with Musset.

SÉCHÉ, LÉON. *Alfred de Musset.* Paris: Mercure de France, 1907, 2 vols. (I, *L'Homme et l'œuvre. Les Camarades;* II, *Les Femmes).* Invaluable particularly for filling in the background of Musset's life with portraits of the men and women who figured most prominently in it.

SOUPAULT, PHILIPPE. *Alfred de Musset.* Paris: Seghers, Collection Poètes d'Aujourd'hui, 1957. Especially interesting in its analyses of Musset's personality and moods.

TILLEY, ARTHUR. *Three French Dramatists.* Cambridge, England: Cambridge University Press, 1933. A comparison of Racine, Marivaux, and Musset.

TONGE, FREDERICK. *L'Art du dialogue dans les comédies en prose d'Alfred de Musset.* Paris: Nizet, 1967. A thorough thesis with detailed analyses. At one point a striking comparison is made between Musset's technique and that of some Romantic composers.

VAN TIEGHEM, PHILIPPE. *Musset, l'homme et l'œuvre.* Paris: Boivin, Le Livre de l'Etudiant, 1944 (new ed., 1957). A penetrating and thought-provoking study.

Index

Index

Index

Musset, Victor de, 13, 14, 16

Napoleon I, 6, 58, 69
Napoleon, Prince, 33
Nodier, Charles, 10, 11, 70, 78, 84
Nodier, Marie, 11

Odinot, Dr Raoul, 26
Olivier, Juste, 2n
Orwell, George, 62

Pagello, Dr Pietro, 21, 22, 23, 24, 25
Paul, Saint, 53
Plato, 63
Pommier, Jean, 19
Pradier, James, 31
Le Provincial, 11
Puccini, Giacomo, 9, 41; La Bohème, 41

Rachel, 27
Racine, Jean, 27, 50, 51, 89, 99, 102, 114, 127; Phèdre, 102
Raine, Kathleen, 6
Revue des Deux Mondes, 16, 17, 37
Ronsard, Pierre de, 4

Sainte-Beuve, Charles-Augustin, 2, 11, 16, 19, 25, 68, 83
Salviati, Cassandra, 4
Sand, George (Baroness Dudevant), 3, 12, 13, 17, 18, 19, 20, 21, 22, 23, 24, 25, 26, 27, 30, 31, 33, 39, 50, 52, 54, 68, 77, 79, 80, 118, 120; Elle et lui, 19, 25, 39; Journal intime, 25; Lettres d'un voyageur, 22
Schiller, Friedrich, 8
Schumann, Robert, 125
Scott, Walter, 46, 92
Séché, Léon, 2n, 3, 4, 5, 30, 31
Shakespeare, William, 8, 90, 91, 93, 99, 103, 128, 129; Hamlet, 125; The Merchant of Venice, 91; A Midsummer Night's Dream, 111; Romeo and Juliet, 24, 113; The Tempest, 129
Sices, David, 113
Soupault, Philippe, 1
Staël, Mme de, 69, 73

Stendhal (Beyle, Henri), 20
Strachey, Lytton, 99
Suberville, Jean, 84

Tattet, Alfred, 13, 25, 28, 30, 33, 79
Le Temps, 16
The Thousand and One Nights, 7
Titian, 40, 45
Tschaikowsky, Pyotr Ilyich, 129

Van Tieghem, Philippe, 48, 128
Velazquez, Diego, 93
Vigny, Alfred de, 2, 11, 14, 35, 53, 64, 65, 85, 86, 88, 89, 115; Chatterton, 64, 88, 115; Le More de Venise, 89

Wailly, Noël-François de, 63
Watteau, Antoine, 127
Wilde, Oscar, The Importance of Being Earnest, 97

DATE DUE

GAYLORD			PRINTED IN U.S.A.